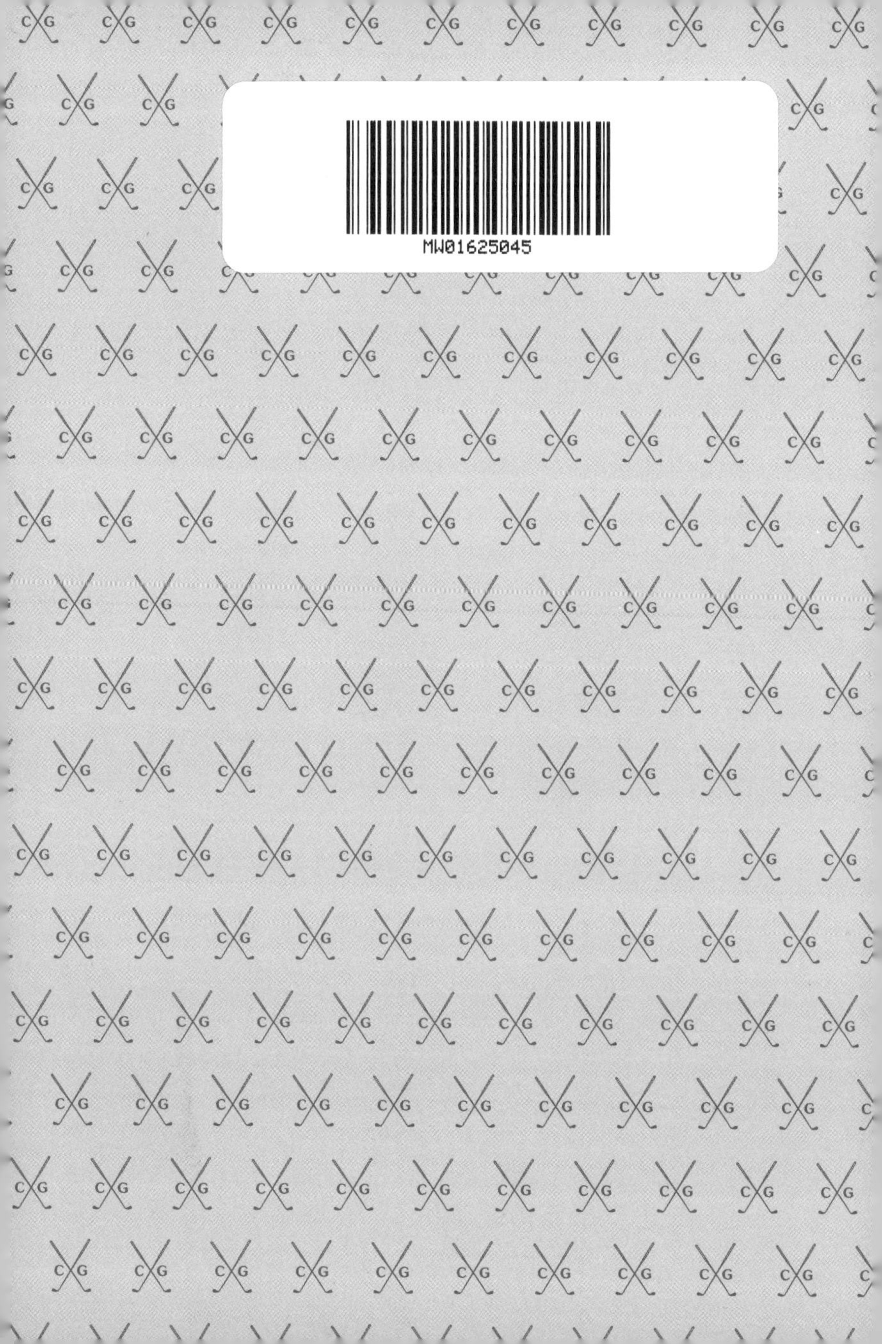
MW01625045

C
G

Dr. MacKenzie on the first tee of one of his masterpieces, the Cypress Point Golf Club, 1930.

THE CLASSICS OF GOLF

Edition of

GOLF ARCHITECTURE

by

Dr. A. MacKenzie

Foreword by Herbert Warren Wind

Afterword by Lewis A. Lapham

Appendix: Cypress Point Golf Club prospectus and map of course.

First published, 1920, Simpkin, Marshall, Hamilton, Kent & Co. Reprinted from an original 1920 edition. The Publisher and Editor wish to thank the Cypress Point Club and especially Bill Borland, Jim Langley, and Lewis Lapham for their assistance in making it possible to reprint the original club prospectus.

ISBN 0-940889-16-1

Foreword

One would imagine that, from the game's earliest days, golfers were as acutely aware of the courses they played as horsemen were of the routes they covered. During the last twenty-five years of the nineteenth century, when golf had become something like the game we know today, increased attention was paid to the elements that made for superior holes and more enjoyable courses. At that time, golf had not spread all around the world, as it was destined to, but its enthusiasts were cognizant that it was unique among games: it was not played on a level floor or field with set dimensions but over natural terrain. They also understood, as did the earlier generations of golfers, that golf was both most appealing and rewarding when it was played on courses laid out on gently rolling land, like the linksland along the sea in St. Andrews. This may have explained, up to a point, why many new golf clubs in Scotland, England, and Ireland frequently sought the services of Old Tom Morris, the custodian of the Old Course at St. Andrews, to design a course for them over the linksland they had purchased for that purpose. To be sure, the members of Dornoch, Newcastle County Down, Westward Ho!, Lahinch, Mac-

rihanish, and the other courses that Old Tom designed also appreciated that he had been a great champion and was known to be a congenial man of perception and worth.

As far back as 1891, the first book about the best golf courses in Great Britain was published. It was written by Horace Hutchinson, the winner of the British Amateur championship in 1886 and 1887, and it was called "Famous Golf Links". In 1910, Bernard Darwin, who had become the golf correspondent of the Times *of London two years earlier, produced his milestone book, "The Golf Courses of the British Isles". Darwin wrote about the championship courses and the other outstanding layouts in Scotland, England, Ireland, and Wales, and Harry Rountree, a New Zealand artist, added his superb watercolor illustrations. "The Golf Courses of the British Isles" was a huge success. Darwin dealt not only with the strong points of championship courses, but he also discussed with his invariable verve dozens of other courses that had a genuine appeal for him because of their singular atmosphere, their beauty, an individual hole of definite originality, or an exceptional run of exciting holes.*

By the turn of the century, golf had already

grown into an important sport, and golf-course architecture was well on its way to becoming a respected and well-paying profession. By that time, courses had to be built inland to satisfy the needs of everyone who wanted to play the game, and it was generally recognized by both golf-course architects and discerning golfers that the most favorable results were achieved when the club's site for its course had the pleasant undulations of linksland. There was also general agreement that more appealing holes could be fashioned on inland courses by moving earth here and there to create more suitable sites for tees, more interesting routes from tee to green, more intriguing hazards, more receptive greens, and a number of good pin positions.

There was an art to it all. The finest inland courses possessed the basic character of the finest linksland courses to a high degree, even when a number of their holes were lined with firs and pines. Their individual holes were essentially as strategic in design as the celebrated holes at St. Andrews, Sandwich, Hoylake, and the other championship links. For example, they rewarded the player who gambled successfully on cutting the corner off the tee on a dogleg par-5 hole, and, as a result, put himself in a position to reach the green on his second shot and to subsequently birdie the hole. Golf holes of strategic design not only encouraged bold play but they also punished the golfer who accepted the challenge that a certain hole presented but failed to produce the required shots. The leaders in golf-course architecture realized early and clearly that an alternate route from tee to green should be presented on every long par-4 and every par-5 hole. This permitted golfers of varying degrees of skill to play the hole in a manner that suited their ability. Golf-course architects quickly came to understand that an inland course built on clayey soil presented many problems they didn't have to worry about when they were working on sandy linksland. On a course with a clay base, an efficient drainage system had to be installed. It was mandatory also for a golf-course architect to have a sufficient knowledge of agronomy to be able to choose the strains of grass that would respond most successfully to the local soil and climate. While golf-course architecture was a glamorous, self-fulfilling profession, it was a difficult one. Its ideal practitioner needed to have the soul of an artist, the brain of an engineer, and the heart of a golfer.

The first books on golf-course architecture written by golf-course architects appeared in the

1920s when golf enjoyed a tremendous boom following the close of the First World War. During that decade, no fewer than seven books on this subject appeared. The first of these, a small but substantial book by Alister MacKenzie called "Golf Architecture", was published in London in 1920. At that time, MacKenzie had not created the three great courses on which his reputation principally rests—Royal Melbourne, in the Sand Belt close to that Australian city; Cypress Point, on the Monterey Peninsula in California, only three or four miles from Pebble Beach; and Augusta National, in Augusta, Georgia, which MacKenzie co-designed with Robert T. "Bobby" Jones, Jr.

"Some Essays on Golf-Course Architecture" by H.S. Colt and C.H. Alison also appeared in 1920. It is a comprehensive study of the state of golf-course architecture on the eve of the game's sudden explosion into international prominence. The partnership of Harry Colt and Hugh Alison was in a class by itself. The partners generally worked on individual projects. Colt had studied law at Cambridge University and had been a solicitor before he designed his first course, Rye, in 1894. He became the secretary at Sunningdale in 1901, but was very active in golf

architecture before and after leaving that post in 1913. He designed many notable courses: the Eden Course, in St. Andrews, and Longniddry in Scotland; the new course at Sunningdale, Stoke Poges, Swinley Forest, St. George's Hill, and Worplesdon in England; Portrush and Rosapenna in Ireland; St. Cloud in France and Real Club de la Puerto de Hierro in Spain. In this country, he assisted George Crump in the development of Pine Valley, the great course in New Jersey. After the First World War, Colt was entrusted with the revision of both Muirfield and Hoylake, and his work on these two historic courses more than justified the confidence placed in him. Alison, a graduate of Oxford, was the club secretary at Stoke Poges at the time when Colt was in the process of building the course. He worked as Colt's assistant until the First World War. Shortly after the close of the war, they formed their partnership. Alison did the major part of his work outside Great Britain. He was responsible for the first modern golf courses in Japan. These included Hirono, near Kobe, and the Tokyo Country Club. He also worked with Kinya Fujita, the designer of Kasumigaseki, to improve that enchanting course. In Australia, he designed the Huntingdale course in the Sand Belt, outside

Melbourne. He was kept very busy in the United States. His American courses include Sea Island, in Georgia; Century and Old Oaks, in New York; Bob O'Link and Highland Park, in Illinois; Burning Tree, in Maryland; Canoe Brook, in New Jersey; and the Milwaukee Country Club, in Wisconsin.

"The Links", by Wiles Robert Hunter, of Indiana, came out in 1926. An intellectual who addressed his energies to the serious social problems of the modern world, Hunter's interest in golf-course architecture began as a change of pace for him, a hobby. In his later years, after he had moved to California, it gradually developed into his chief pursuit. During this period, he was closely in touch with MacKenzie and other architects, and took an active interest in their projects. "The Links" is an extended essay in which Hunter discusses the qualities a course must possess in order to measure up to the highest possible standards. His point of view was sound, and he projected it energetically.

The following year, 1927, saw the publication of "Golf Architecture in America: Its Strategy and Construction", by George C. Thomas, Jr. The son of a well-to-do and socially prominent Philadelphia family, Thomas, after graduating from the University of Pennsylvania, worked in banking for a few years, but in 1907 he decided to devote his time to his real passion, gardening in general and the breeding of roses in particular. Golf-course architecture attracted him, and he was an interested observer of the courses that Donald Ross, A.W. Tillinghast, and Hugh Wilson were then building in and around Philadelphia. Thomas himself designed what is now the course of the Whitemarsh Valley Country Club on his family's estate in Chestnut Hill, on the edge of the city. After serving in the Army Air Corps in Europe in the First World War, Thomas on his return hearkened to the call of California. There, in the 1920s, he designed many fine golf courses, including four really wonderful ones in Greater Los Angeles: the North and South Courses of the Los Angeles Country Club; Bel-Air Country Club in the Bel-Air district of the sprawling city; and Riviera Country Club, in Pacific Palisades, not far from the ocean. This quartet has stood the test of time very well. It is a pity that Thomas's book on golf architecture does not evoke the personality of this fascinating man and his significant accomplishments in golf-course architecture.

In 1928, an important book largely about golf-course architecture appeared: Charles

Blair Macdonald's autobiography, "Scotland's Gift—Golf" . Macdonald, the first United States Amateur champion—he won the title in 1895—had attended St. Andrews University, and, not being of a modest nature, he somehow felt that this entitled him to personally dictate the development of American golf. He did, however, build the first great American course, the National Golf Links, in Southampton, Long Island. Macdonald had a splendid understanding of the playing values that one-shot, two-shot, and three-shot holes should possess, for his early years in St. Andrews had given him a remarkable sense of strategic architecture. Along with this, Macdonald had the wisdom when working on his later projects to always have at his side a trained engineer, a Seth Raynor or a Charles Banks, to help solve the involved problems which presented themselves at many sites, such as the Mid-Ocean Club in Bermuda, the Lido Golf Club off the south shore of Long Island, and the Ray Tompkins Memorial course, the Yale Golf Club, in the wild, rugged acreage north of New Haven. The National Golf Links was undoubtedly the most valuable contribution that C.B. Macdonald made to American golf. One weekend at the National, and the visiting committee from a new golf club in Buffalo or Cedar Rapids or Nashville or Austin or Spokane had a much deeper understanding of the kind of golf holes they should strive to build back home.

The last in this sudden eruption of books on golf-course architecture in the 1920s was "The Architectural Side of Golf", written by two Englishmen, H.N. Wethered, and Thomas Simpson. It was published in London in 1929. Simpson, a golf-course architect, built such first-rate courses as Chantilly, Morfontaine, and Royal Madrid on the continent, along with Cruden Bay (near Aberdeen) and Berkshire in Britain. Wethered, who knew his way about golf very well, brought out "The Perfect Golfer", a series of extended essays, in 1931. Simpson possessed exceptional discipline, as golf-course architects go. In the 1930s, when he was called in by the Ballybunion Golf Club, in southwestern Ireland, to look over its still largely unknown course and to suggest improvements, Simpson had the uncommon good sense to appreciate that Ballybunion was one of the best and most awesome courses in the world. There were only four holes, he thought, which could be improved. Once he had altered them and made them not only stronger but subtler, Simpson was on his way again. One can understand why he was so often asked to do revisions of courses that already enjoyed a high reputation.

For some reason, many of the books briefly discussed above and most of the others that have been written in more recent times by golf-course architects have neither been as instructive nor as entertaining as their readers had hoped for. One explanation may be that golf-course architects tend to be such fluent, beguiling talkers when they describe courses they expect to complete in a matter of months that you feel another Merion is in the works. In this context, during the last twenty-five years or so, the most successful golf-course architects have been so busy making every golden moment count that, instead of writing thoughtful books, which is time-consuming, they happily go along with the exuberant press releases sent out by the public relations firms engaged by the golf clubs. One of the ironies of the prosperous post-Second World War era, when so many clubs wanted to built superlatively good courses and damn the expense, is that only a handful of admirable courses emerged. The architects had so many scattered projects on their agenda that they could not find the time to stay put at any one course during the crucial weeks, and sometimes months, when rough ideas are translated into holes that really play. Another thing that took place during this period is that golfers in this country gained a much greater respect for courses that had been constructed relatively early in this century—Seminole, Cypress Point, Ekwanok, the Lake Course at Olympic, Pine Valley, Maidstone, Chicago Golf, San Francisco Golf, the Cascades Course at Hot Springs, Pebble Beach, Kittansett, Shinnecock Hills, the composite course at The Country Club, and Riviera, to name a few that come quickly to mind.

Before returning to Alister MacKenzie and "Golf Architecture", this is probably as good a time as any to note that two magnificent books on the subject have come out in the last dozen years, "The World Atlas of Golf", published in 1976, and "The Golf Course", published in 1981. The British publishing firm of Mitchell Beazley along with Pat Ward-Thomas, Charles Price, and Peter Thomson are the people chiefly responsible for the "World Atlas", which offers accurate, full-color maps in addition to informed writing, photographs, and assorted illustrations of seventy of the best golf courses in the world—twenty-five of them in the United Kingdom, Ireland, and continental Europe; twenty-seven in Canada, the United States,

Mexico, Bermuda, and the Caribbean; eight in Asia; five in Australia and New Zealand; three in Africa; and two in South America. The history and lore of each course is covered in detail, as are the players and the tournaments associated with it. There are smaller but no less excellent depictions of the layouts of another hundred of the world's leading courses, supplemented with brief, adroit descriptions of their architectural qualities. This is an indispensable volume. "The Golf Course", published by the Rutledge Press, is the work of Geoffrey S. Cornish, the well-known golf-course architect, whose main office is in Amherst, Massachusetts, and Ronald E. Whitten, an attorney, who lives in Silver Lake, Kansas. Whitten is a golf scholar who has researched the history of golf-course architecture with an unprecedented thoroughness and brilliance. "The Golf Course" is copiously illustrated with photographs and drawings, and it has an invaluable section called Profiles, an alphabetical listing of golf-course architects, past and present, and a detailed account of their work. It is a considerable contribution to golf.

For many of us, Alister MacKenzie's "Golf Architecture" is the most informative and interesting of the early books on golf-course archi-

tecture written by a member of that profession. Before proceeding further, it should be brought out that it has never been established once and for all whether MacKenzie's name should be spelled MacKenzie or Mackenzie. It appears as Mackenzie on the cover of his book, but in this foreword I am going with MacKenzie. That has been my practice ever since I found his name signed that way on the classic map of the Old Course at St. Andrews that he surveyed and depicted, and which was brought out by W.C. Henderson & Son, Ltd., University Press, St. Andrews, in 1924. That map now hangs on the walls of countless offices, studies, and dens around the world. Had I come across "Golf Architecture" prior to the map of St. Andrews, I am sure I would be using Mackenzie. The spelling of his name fluctuated throughout his life—a most unusual one.

Alister MacKenzie was born in Leeds, in Yorkshire, in 1870, the son of a Scottish doctor from the Highlands who practiced in that city. (Alister is the Scottish spelling of Alistair.) A man with a wide-ranging mind, he went to Cambridge University, where he received degrees in medicine, chemistry, and natural science. He decided to practice medicine, and joined his father's office in Leeds. (Technically,

I suppose, we should be addressing MacKenzie as Dr. MacKenzie, as many people do.) When the Boer War broke out, MacKenzie served as a surgeon with the Somerset Light Infantry. In view of the direction his life later took, it should be noted that during the war he was deeply impressed by the Boers use of camouflage in the open field to disguise their military positions and their deployment of troops. At the close of the war, he returned to Leeds and to the life of a general practitioner of medicine. In 1907, significantly, he was a member of the group in Leeds that founded the Alwoodley Golf Club and selected Harry Colt to build a course for the club on an attractive moorland property outside the city. As the honorary secretary of the club, MacKenzie had already immersed himself in golf-course architecture. Colt liked many of his thoughts on how to use the acreage at Alwoodley, and the result was that Colt and MacKenzie worked in close concert as they laid out eighteen holes over that fine stretch of moorland which is punctuated with heather and gorse. A number of MacKenzie's suggestions for the use of certain natural features reflected his background in camouflage. It surprised few of MacKenzie's friends when, shortly after Alwoodley was completed, he undertook the construction of Moortown, a course situated close by and on the same kind of land. Moortown, incidentally, was the venue of the Ryder Cup match in 1929.

This budding new career of MacKenzie's was interrupted by the outbreak of the First World War. He was called up and given the rank of major in the Army Medical Corps. He did not wish to serve as a medical officer during the war, for he believed that he could make a more valuable contribution in the field of camouflage. It was somehow arranged that Major MacKenzie of the Army Medical Corps could become Lieutenant MacKenzie of the Royal Engineers. His first project, which was undertaken on a parcel of land close by the Moortown course, gave him ample opportunity to experiment with the camouflaging of trenches and other earthworks. Some officer of high rank must have liked what he saw, because MacKenzie's next assignment took him to London. There, in Hyde Park, he became the very active head of a school of camouflage that was attended by officers of the British Army and allied forces. He was later dispatched to France to serve as the camouflage expert for a British Army corps. After the Armistice, he headed home to Leeds again, but by this time he knew that neither medicine nor camouflage held quite as much fascination for him as golf-course architecture. He quickly found work in that field in Britain, wrote his thesis, "Golf Architecture", and in the early 1920s headed for the United States where he worked mainly with Charles Alison and Perry Maxwell.

MacKenzie's most renowned work was done from the mid-1920s on. Late in 1926, he was called on to design Royal Melbourne. He was assisted in this project by Alex Russell, a former Australian Open champion, who had become a golf-course architect. MacKenzie had at his disposal an ideal tract of tumbling duneland, some of it wooded. He made the most of it. Almost every hole presents the golfer with an appealing problem to solve. On the second hole, for example, should he try on his tee shot to carry the many-fingered, gleaming white bunker on the right side of the fairway on this short par 5 of 480 yards which runs uphill to a slippery green that slopes every which way? On the sixth, a 428-yard par 4 that doglegs sharply to the right and then sweeps up to a temperamental green bordered by tea trees and she-oaks, how much of the corner should he try to bite off? There is ample reason to be conservative, for several steep-walled bunkers are tucked together in the angle of the dogleg. If the pin is set back on the upper terrace of the green, the golfer must make certain that he puts plenty of backspin on his lofted approach shot or else elects to play a pitch-and-run shot. The eighth is a par 4 that measures only 305 yards. The inviting fairway slides in a long arc to the left, but to reach it the golfer must carry a somewhat deceptive bunker that eases along it for yards and yards. After a first-rate drive, all he is asked to do is play a well-judged pitch to a small, twisty green. If a golfer plays a sturdy round on Royal Melbourne, it gives him immense satisfaction, for he has had to think his way around a demanding course and come up with a succession of well-played shots.

Royal Melbourne is the course that made MacKenzie's reputation. It is also the story of a fruitful collaboration. Alex Russell's suggestions patently put a sharper edge on a few of MacKenzie's conceptions. After the MacKenzie course, the West Course, was completed, Russell later built another eighteen, the East Course. It is filled with tasteful holes that have the same spirit and flavor as the ones on the West. On Royal Melbourne's Composite Course, which is used only on special occasions such as the 1959 Canada Cup (later World Cup) Match, six holes from the East Course are combined with twelve from the West. Hogan hasn't played it, but he would love it. All the holes at Royal Melbourne benefited immeasurably from the assiduous attention that Claude Crockford, an unusually gifted greenkeeper, lavished on them. He and his successors deserve especial credit for the work that they have done to keep the marvelous greens healthy and fast.

Since relatively few golfers from Britain and the United States got to play Royal Melbourne in the days before worldwide air travel, the course that made everybody in the game aware of MacKenzie's immense talents was Cypress Point. After the death of Seth Raynor, the first choice of the organizing committee at Cypress Point, MacKenzie was selected to design the course. In 1926 he had become well enough acquainted with its spectacular one hundred and seventy acres to arrive at a routing plan that underwent only minor changes before work on building the course was begun. In the Afterword of this book, Lewis A. Lapham, who was intimately involved in the genesis of Cypress Point, discusses in detail the history and character of the course and the club. There is no need to describe them further here except to note that MacKenzie made the most of the thrilling and diverse natural terrain in his routing of the eighteen holes. Because of their proximity and their majestic headlands high above the Pacific, the individual qualities of Cypress Point and Pebble Beach are often discussed. I remain amazed at the ingenuous routing plan that Jack Neville came up with at Pebble Beach, and MacKenzie's routing of the holes at Cypress Point is no less stunning.

In 1929 the United States Amateur championship was played at Pebble Beach. Bobby Jones, the defending champion, was one of the men in the Amateur field who had heard that Cypress Point, recently completed, was a terrific course. It was arranged for him to play it before the start of the Amateur. He was enchanted with it. In the Amateur, Jones was defeated in the first round by Johnny Goodman, 1 up. I have no idea whether or not Jones played Cypress Point again after his quick elimination, but the impression the course made on him was a lasting one. In September, 1930, Jones completed his Grand Slam of the British and American Open and Amateur championships by winning our Amateur in late September. Shortly after this, he announced his retirement from competition. He was then in a position to build the dream course he had long thought about. He found the plot of land he wanted in Augusta, Georgia. He wanted to work on the design of the course with a professional architect as co-designer. He chose MacKenzie, I would guess, largely because of his high regard for Cypress Point.

Jones and MacKenzie started work on the Augusta National Golf Club's course in 1931. It was opened for play in 1933. On their first exploratory walks around the property—it had previously been the site of one of the leading nurseries in the South—Jones and MacKenzie were both astonished when they saw, at the base of the very long hill below the clubhouse, that long, swinging, almost semi-circular sweep of land that became the thirteenth. They instantly realized that here was a great natural golf hole just waiting to be discovered. When the Masters tournament was inaugurated in 1934, the fairways and greens at the Augusta National were much harder and faster than they later became. Jones was a profound admirer of the linksland courses in Britain, and while he understood that at Augusta they were working not with a sandy base but with clay soil, he wanted a number of the holes to present the same kind of test that the best linksland holes do. During the Second World War, the club was closed and the land was used for grazing. When the first post-war Masters took place in 1946, it was observable that the fairways and greens had lost much of their former firmness and speed. The Augusta National yielded to its apparent destiny and became the most beautiful meadowland course in the world. In the fall of 1980, in an effort to get firmer greens, the club decided to take out their old Bermuda-grass base and to plant an advanced strain of bent grass. In 1987, finally, the new greens had a very healthy growth, and the combination of an almost rainless winter, the skill of a new superintendent who knew bent grass well, and a patch of dry, windy weather resulted in firm, linksland greens for the Masters.

In retrospect, it is easy to see that MacKenzie and Jones were a very good team. Courses that are built on the side of a long hill are rarely successful. Augusta National is because, as the vast natural amphitheater slides downhill to its stage, the twelfth green, Jones and MacKenzie saw to it that on only one hole, the fourteenth, is there the suggestion that the golfer is playing a sidehill hole. Rae's Creek and its tributaries were used with imagination, as were the magnificent stands of pine. The routing of holes is truly astonishing. No two consecutive holes head in the same direction. On the first nine, for that matter, no two consecutive holes have the same par. The sequence is 454 343 454. Incidentally, on the first, third, and fourth holes, the scores for the Masters field in relation to par run very high.

When one thinks back over Alister MacKenzie's life and all he managed to accomplish, it is saddening to learn that he did not live long enough to enjoy the huge acclamation Augusta National received when the first Masters was held there in 1934. He had died the previous January in Pasatiempo, California. He had come to that pleasant town to build a golf course, and he subsequently decided to make his home there. MacKenzie was only sixty-four when he died, but he had certainly packed a lot of doing into his life.

Had MacKenzie lived longer, the chances are that things would have gone differently than they did and that he would have, for example, been spared the anguish of discovering how badly his plans for the two courses he had designed for the Jockey Club of Buenos Aires had miscarried. The courses were opened for play in 1935. Patently, the chief of the construction crew knew nothing about golf, and apparently no officer at the club was sufficiently informed about golf-course architecture to pre-

vent the blundering. The mounds, hillocks, and undulations that were meant to give a sense of movement to the club's flat-as-the-pampas acreage were—and still are—terribly artificial. Only a few of the bunkers have the look of a MacKenzie bunker, and the greens are routinely flat and dull. The beautiful specimen trees and shrubs, which were meant to give the holes definition, stand as stiff and staid as strangers in a foreign land. Too often the Jockey Club is referred to as one of MacKenzie's triumphs. Not at all. There are many better golf courses in Buenos Aires.

When "Golf Architecture" was published in 1920, Alister MacKenzie was fifty. His exceptional talent as a golf-course architect was recognized by his fellow British architects, but his international reputation was meager. He had built some excellent courses in northern England, but he had yet to come up with a celebrated course. He had thought seriously about golf architecture for some twenty years and was convinced that the elements of strategic design, which made the Old Course at St. Andrews the finest golf course in the world, were the basis of creating a first-class course either by the sea or well inland, or, indeed, any place where eighteen holes could be built. However, do not expect "Golf Architecture" to be a charming literary adventure. It is primarily the work of a man who is trying to get down on paper his ideas, some obvious and other recondite, about the multiple considerations that go into designing and maintaining a sound, stimulating course that both the professional and the average golfer will enjoy playing.

"Golf Architecture" is divided into four chapters: General Principles of Economy in Course Construction and Green-keeping; Some Further Suggestions; Ideal Holes; and The Future of Golf Architecture. Early in the first chapter, MacKenzie enumerates the essential features of an ideal golf course. Here are the first three:

> *1. The course, where possible, should be arranged in two loops of nine holes.*
>
> *2. There should be a large proportion of good two-shot holes, two or three drive-and-pitch holes, and at least four one-shot holes.*
>
> *3. There should be little walking between the greens and the tees, and the course should be arranged so that in the first instance there is always a slight walk forwards from the green to the next tee; then the holes are sufficiently elastic to be lengthened in the future if necessary.*

There are thirteen of these "essential features" in MacKenzie's list. Some of them are relatively commonplace, but others go to the heart of golf-course design. They were guide-posts for MacKenzie throughout his career. In his third and fourth chapters, MacKenzie deals further with these "essential features". In the opening chapter, however, his writing is about practical matters most of the way, as if he were addressing the green committee of a hard-pressed golf club which was in dire need of a specialist's advice. He wished to emphasize some fundamental points, such as these:

> *The chief object of every golf architect or green-keeper worth his salt is to imitate the beauties of nature so closely as to make his work indistinguishable from nature itself.*
>
> *Most golfers have an entirely erroneous view of the real object of hazards. The majority of them simply look upon hazards as a means of punishing a bad shot, when their real object is to make the game interesting.*
>
> *Hazards should be placed with an object, and none should be made which has not some influence on the line of play to the hole.*
>
> *On many courses there are far too many bunkers: the sides of the fairway are riddled with them, and many of these courses would be equally interesting if half of the bunkers were turfed over as grassy hollows.*
>
> *On a seaside course in particular little construction work is necessary; the most important thing is to make the fullest possible use of existing features.*

As he gets deeper into his extended opening

chapter, MacKenzie begins to view the reader as if the latter were indubitably a practicing greenkeeper. He tells him how to get rid of worms in his soil, how to order the right kind of artificial manure to correct certain problems, and why greens should continue to be mowed in the winter. As long as the reader doesn't actually have to do the work, it is pleasant to add to one's knowledge. At about this point in the book, MacKenzie leavens his prose from time to time with Scottish humor, and he also reminds us frequently that in the costly world of 1920 one must watch his pennies.

In the second chapter, MacKenzie continues to address the reader as a dedicated, prudent greenkeeper as he goes into the most intelligent ways to deal with carting, draining, seeding, turfing, manuring, sanding, and other such problems in the maintenance of a golf course. The reader can skip through this chapter if he finds it heavy going. MacKenzie's conscientiousness is impressive, though. His goal of striving to create testing but natural-looking holes could not be more different from that of many modern golf-course architects who are adding to the plethora of strange new courses now finding a place on the P.G.A. Tour.

In the third chapter, Ideal Holes, MacKenzie

goes into intricate detail on the merits of the strategic school of golf-course architecture, the best approach to the game by far. A hole of strategic design asks the golfer to make his way from tee to green by playing to the left or right of a hazard unless he is able to carry it. MacKenzie spells out his main point very clearly.

> *The difficulties that make a hole really interesting are usually those in which a great advantage can be gained in successfully accomplishing heroic carries over hazards of an impressive appearance, or in taking great risks in placing a shot so as to gain a big advantage for the next . . . At first sight he [the golfer] looks upon it as grossly unfair that, of two tee shots within a few inches of each other, the one should be hopelessly buried in a bunker and the other should be in an ideal position.*
>
> *However, on further consideration he will realize that, as in dog-legged holes, this is the chief characteristic of all good holes.*
>
> *Holes of this description not only cater for great judgment, but great skill: a man who has such confidence that he can place his ball within a few feet of his objective gains a big advantage over his opponent who dare not take similar risks.*

Here is another well-expressed approach to the core of strategic golf-course architecture:

> *An ideal golf hole should provide an infinite variety of shots according to the various positions of the tee, the*

situation of the flag, the direction and strength of the wind, etc.

MacKenzie nominates the eleventh at St. Andrews, which is a par 3 of a hundred and seventy-two yards, as an ideal one-shot hole, mainly because it offers a fair challenge to golfers of all degrees of skill. He considers the 170-yard eighth hole at Moortown, a course he designed, a strategically sound par 3. The narrow entrance to its green is guarded on both sides by bunkers, and a ball that lands on the natural slope just before the green almost invariably kicks into one of the hazards. (A photograph and a sketch of this hole, which is called Gibraltar, are included.) The ideal two-shot and three-shot holes that pop quickly into MacKenzie's mind are the justly renowned sixteenth, seventeenth, and fourteenth holes on the Old Course at St. Andrews. He describes in loving detail the factors that make these holes such intriguing tests of a player's course management, composure, and shotmaking ability. There are sketches of these three wonderful holes, which play as well today as they did in 1920. MacKenzie also describes his design that won the ideal two-shot hole competition that Country Life *magazine held in 1914. A sketch of MacKenzie's hole is included, and it nicely depicts the five different routes to the green that a golfer can choose to take. I wonder which holes MacKenzie would have selected from Augusta National as ideal holes. He would cite the thirteenth almost surely, I believe. Probably the twelfth, too. After that, I am not certain. Maybe the third. One must bear in mind that many of the holes on Augusta National have been altered, some of them drastically, since 1934.*

In the fourth and final chapter, The Future of Golf Architecture, MacKenzie gets off his chest a number of personal opinions that range from how surely the late-Victorian type of inland course offends all the finest instincts of the artist and the sportsman to a brisk discussion of the attributes that a successful golf-course architect and a highly skilled camoufleur share. Here are a few provocative MacKenzieisms:

> *A good golf course is a great asset to a nation. Those who harangue about land being diverted from agriculture and used for golf have little sense of proportion. Comparing the small amount of land utilised for golf with the large amount devoted to agriculture, we get infinitely more value out of the former than the latter. We all eat too much.*
>
> *How frequently have I, with great difficulty, persuaded patients who were never off my doorstep to take*

up golf, and how rarely, if ever, have I seen them in my consulting-rooms again!

The test of a good golf architect is the power of converting bad inland material into a good course, and not the power of fashioning excellent seaside material into a mediocre one.

The ideal golf architect should have made a study, from a golfing point of view, of agricultural chemistry, botany, and geology. He should also have some knowledge of surveying, map-reading, and the interpretation of aerial photographs.

I believe that the real reason St. Andrews Old Course is infinitely superior to anything else is owing to the fact that it was constructed when no one knew anything about the subject at all, and since then it has been considered too sacred to be touched.

One doesn't always have to agree with Alister MacKenzie, but a man who designed three such great courses as Royal Melbourne, Cypress Point, and Augusta National is well worth listening to.

Herbert Warren Wind

THE 140-YARD SHORT HOLE AT SITWELL PARK: a fiercely criticised green that has become universally popular.

Frontispiece]

GOLF ARCHITECTURE

ECONOMY IN COURSE CONSTRUCTION AND GREEN-KEEPING

BY

DR. A. MACKENZIE

WITH AN INTRODUCTION

BY

H. S. COLT

SIMPKIN, MARSHALL, HAMILTON,
KENT & CO. LTD., 4 STATIONERS'
HALL COURT : : LONDON, E.C.4

First published 1920

INTRODUCTION

My partner, who is the author of these short essays on Golf Course Architecture, has asked me to write an introduction. This is, however, hardly necessary, as the name of Dr. Mackenzie is so well known in connection with this subject.

Many years ago now the idea came to him, as to a few others, that it might not be impossible to create a golf course without doing damage to the natural attractions of the site. Up to that period the courses which had been designed by man, and not by nature, had in great measure failed in this direction, and although no doubt they had provided necessary opportunities for playing the game, the surroundings in many cases proved a source of irritation rather than pleasure.

I vividly remember meeting my present partner for the first time. I had been asked to go to Leeds to advise about the design of the Alwoodley Golf Course, and stayed at his house. After dinner he took me into his consulting room, where, instead of finding myself surrounded by the weapons of his profession as a Doctor of Medicine, I sat in the midst of a collection of photographs of sand bunkers, putting greens, and golf courses, and many plans and designs of the Alwoodley Course. I found that I was staying with a real enthusiast, and one who had already given close attention to a subject in which I have always been interested.

And it is this enthusiasm for the natural beauty of nature which has helped him in all his work, so that in the case of Alwoodley the player not only has the opportunity of displaying his skill in the game, but also of enjoying the relaxation which delightful natural surroundings always give

No doubt many mistakes were made in our early attempts, and I never visit a course which I have designed without seeing where improvements could be made in the constructional work, and as long as this is so, I feel that we shall all continue to learn and to make progress, our instructor being nature herself.

H. S. Colt.

CONTENTS

ILLUSTRATIONS

Illustrations

GOLF ARCHITECTURE

CHAPTER I

GENERAL PRINCIPLES OF ECONOMY IN COURSE CONSTRUCTION AND GREEN-KEEPING

Economy in course construction consists in obtaining the best possible results at a minimum of cost. The more one sees of golf courses, the more one realises the importance of doing construction work really well, so that it is likely to be of a permanent character. It is impossible to lay too much stress on the importance of finality.

Every golfer knows examples of courses which have been constructed and re-arranged over and over again, and the fact that all over the country thousands of pounds are frittered away in doing bad work which will ultimately have to be scrapped is particularly distressful to a true economist. As an example of unnecessary labour and expense, the writer has in mind a green which has been entirely relaid on four different occasions. In the first instance, it was of the ridge and furrow type; the turf was then lifted and it was made dead flat. A new secretary was appointed, and he made it a more pronounced ridge and furrow than ever; it was then relaid and made flat again, and has now been entirely reconstructed with undulations of a more natural outline and appearance.

In discussing the question of finality, it is well to inquire if there are any really first-class courses in existence which have been unaltered for a considerable number of years and still remain, not only a good test of golf, but a source of pleasure to all classes of players. Is there any existing course which not even the rubber cored ball has spoilt? And, if so, what is the cause of its abiding popularity? The only one I know of is one which has been described as "a much-abused old course at a little place called St. Andrews, in the Kingdom of Fife." This (as well as some of the other championship courses to a lesser extent) still retains its popularity among all classes of amateurs. In fact, it is characteristic of all the best courses that they are just as pleasurable (possibly even more so) to the long handicap man as to the player of championship rank. This fact knocks on the head the argument which is often used that the modern expert tries to spoil the pleasure of the player by making courses too difficult.

The successful negotiation of difficulties is a source of pleasure to all classes of players.

It may be asked, "Who originally constructed St. Andrews?" Its origin appears to be shrouded in mystery: like Topsy, in *Uncle Tom's Cabin,* it simply "growed." But the fact of the matter is that St. Andrews differs from others in that it has always been deemed a sacrilege to interfere with its natural beauties, and it has been left almost untouched for centuries. No green-keeper has ever dared to shave down its natural undulations. Most of the bunkers have been left where nature placed them, and others have originated from the winds and the rains enlarging divot marks left by the players, and some of them possibly by the green-keepers converting those hollows where most players congregated, into bunkers, owing to the difficulty of keeping them free from divot marks. The bunkers at St. Andrews are thus placed in positions where players are most likely to go—in fact, in the precise positions which the ordinary Green Committee would suggest should be filled up. This is a significant fact, and tends to show that many of our existing ideas in regard to hazards have been erroneous. Mr. John L. Low pointed out years ago that no hazard is unfair wherever it is placed, and this particularly applies if the hazard is visible, as it should be obvious that if a player sees a hazard in front of him and promptly planks his ball into it he has chosen the wrong spot.

I once heard a Yorkshire tale of an old farmer finding a man in his coal-house during a recent coal strike. He put his head through the window and said, "Now I've copped you picking out all the big lumps." A voice from the darkness came, "You're a liar, I'm taking them as they come."

On the old type of course like St. Andrews, the players have to take the hazards as they come, and do their best to avoid them.

There is nothing new about the ideas

of the so-called Golf Architect : he simply wishes to reproduce the old ideas as exemplified in the old natural courses like St. Andrews, those courses which were played on before over-zealous green committees demolished the natural undulations of the fairways and greens, and made greens like lawns for croquet, tennis, or anything else except golf, and erected eyesores in the shape of straight lines of cop bunkers, instead of emphasising the natural curves of the links.

In the old view of golf, there was no main thoroughfare to the hole : the player had to use his own judgment without the aid of guide posts, or other adventitious means of finding his way. St. Andrews still retains the old traditions of golf. For example, I have frequently seen four individuals playing the long hole (the fourteenth), and deliberately attacking it in four different ways, and three out of the four were probably right in playing it in the ways they selected.

At St. Andrews " it needs a heid to play gowf," as the caddie said to the professor.

As the truest economy consists in finality, it is interesting to consider the essential features of an ideal golf course. Some of them are suggested now :

1. The course, where possible, should be arranged in two loops of nine holes.

2. There should be a large proportion of good two-shot holes, two or three drive-and-pitch holes, and at least four one-shot holes.

3. There should be little walking between the greens and tees, and the course should be arranged so that in the first instance there is always a slight walk forwards from the green to the next tee; then the holes are sufficiently elastic to be lengthened in the future if necessary.

4. The greens and fairways should be

sufficiently undulating, but there should be no hill climbing.

5. Every hole should have a different character.

6. There should be a minimum of blindness for the approach shots.

7. The course should have beautiful surroundings, and all the artificial features should have so natural an appearance that a stranger is unable to distinguish them from nature itself.

8. There should be a sufficient number of heroic carries from the tee, but the course should be arranged so that the weaker player with the loss of a stroke or portion of a stroke shall always have an alternative route open to him.

9. There should be infinite variety in the strokes required to play the various holes—viz., interesting brassy shots, iron shots, pitch and run-up shots.

10. There should be a complete absence of the annoyance and irritation caused

by the necessity of searching for lost balls.

11. The course should be so interesting that even the plus man is constantly stimulated to improve his game in attempting shots he has hitherto been unable to play.

12. The course should be so arranged that the long handicap player, or even the absolute beginner, should be able to enjoy his round in spite of the fact that he is piling up a big score.

13. The course should be equally good during winter and summer, the texture of the greens and fairways should be perfect, and the approaches should have the same consistency as the greens.

A DECIDED ADVANTAGE

In regard to the first three principles, there can be little difference of opinion. It is a considerable advantage that a course should be arranged in two loops of nine holes, as on a busy day players can commence at either the first or tenth tee.

In regard to the fourth principle. It used to be a common fallacy that greens should be made dead flat. Even on some of the best golf courses at the present day you find them made like croquet lawns. There has been somewhat of a reaction lately against undulating greens, but this, I believe, is entirely due to the fact that the undulations have been made of a wrong character, either composed of finicky little humps or of the ridge and furrow type. Natural undulations are the exact opposite to the artificial ridge and furrow. The latter has a narrow hollow, and a broad ridge, whereas the former has a large, bold, sweeping hollow, and a narrow ridge.

The most interesting putting the writer has ever seen is on the Ladies' Putting Course at St. Andrews. Even first-class golfers consider it a privilege to be

THE SIXTEENTH GREEN AT HEADINGLEY, LEEDS—APPROXIMATE COST £50: an entirely artificial hole; the site was originally on a severe downhill slope and had to be cut out of rock

invited there, and are to be found putting with the greatest enthusiasm from early morn till late at night. There the undulations are of the boldest possible type, large sweeping hollows rising abruptly four or five feet up to small plateaus. A modern golf architect who dared to produce the boldness of these St. Andrews' undulations could hardly hope to escape hostile criticism.

In constructing natural-looking undulations one should attempt to study the manner in which those among the sand-dunes are formed. These are fashioned by the wind blowing up the sand in the form of waves, which become gradually turfed over in the course of time. Natural undulations are, therefore, of a similar shape to the waves one sees by the seashore, and are of all kinds of shapes and sizes, but are characterised by the fact that the hollows between the waves are broader than the waves themselves.

If undulations are made of this kind, then there are always plenty of comparatively flat places where the greenkeeper can put the flag, and there should never be any necessity to cut the hole on a slope.

A test of a good undulation is that it should be easy to use the mowing machine over it.

If undulations are made of the kind I describe, it is hardly possible to make them too large or too bold.

Perhaps the most aggravating type of undulation is the finicky little hump or side-slope which you don't see until after you have missed your putt, and then begin to wonder why it has not gone in the hole.

An almost equally common delusion is that fairways should be flat. I quite agree that there is nothing worse than a fairway on a severe side-slope, but, on the other hand, there are few things

THE HOME GREEN AT SITWELL PARK: An undulating green with a wide choice of places for the hole in the hollows or on the flat.

more monotonous than playing every shot from a dead flat fairway. The unobservant player never seems to realise that one of the chief charms of the best seaside links is the undulating fairways, such as those near the club-house at Deal, part of Sandwich, and most of the old course at St. Andrews, where the ground is a continual roll from the first tee to the last green, and where one never has the same shot to play twice ; on these fairways one hardly ever has a level stance or a level lie. It is this that makes the variety of a seaside course, and variety is everything in golf.

If one considers St. Andrews hole by hole, it is surprising to find at how many of them the dominating and important incident is associated with an insignificant-looking hollow or bank, often running obliquely to the line of your approach.

In constructing undulations of this kind on inland courses, it is well to make them with as much variety as possible, and in the direction you wish the player to go to keep the fairway comparatively flat, so as to encourage players to place their shots, and thus get in a favourable position for their next.

In this connection plasticine is frequently used for making models of undulations. Plasticine is useful to teach the green-keeper points in construction he would not otherwise understand—in fact, I believe, I was the first designer of golf courses to use it for this purpose. The 14th green at Alwoodley, which was the first one made there, was constructed from a model in plasticine. It has its disadvantages, however, as a course constructed entirely from models in plasticine has always an artificial appearance, and can never be done as cheaply as one in which the green-keeper is allowed a comparatively free hand in modelling the undulations in such a manner that not only do they harmonise with their surroundings, but are constructed according to the various changes in the subsoil discovered whilst doing the work.

THE FOLLY OF FASHIONS

In regard to the fifth principle that every hole should have a different character. A common mistake is to follow prevailing fashions. At first we had the artificial cop bunkers extending in a dead straight line from the rough on one side to the rough on the other; in modern course architecture these are fortunately extinct. Secondly, we had the fashion of pot bunkers running down each side of the course. This was, if anything, an even more objectionable type of golf than the last. Thirdly, we have had what has been called the alpinisation of golf courses.

In this connection I would point out that green-keepers should be careful not to make hillocks so high in the direct line to the hole that they block out the view: a little to one side of the bee line they may be made as high as one pleases, but in the direct line hollows should, as a rule, take the place of hillocks. This is the exact opposite to what is found on many golf courses, where the hollows are at the sides and the banks in the middle.

The great thing in constructing golf courses is to ensure variety and make everything look natural. The greatest compliment that can be paid to a green-keeper is for players to think his artificial work is natural. On Alwoodley and Moortown practically every green and every hummock has been artificially made, and yet it is difficult to convince the stranger that this is so. I remember a chairman of the Green Committee of one of the best-known clubs in the North telling me that it would be impossible to make

Artificial hummock at Moortown, constructed from the stones removed from the fairway.

their course anything like Alwoodley, as there we had such a wealth of natural hillocks, hollows, and undulations. It was only with great difficulty that I was able to persuade him that, to use an Irishism, these natural features which he so much admired had all been artificially created. I have even heard one of the members of our own Green Committee telling a well-known writer on golf that the hummocks surrounding one of our greens had always been there: he himself had forgotten that he had been present when the site for them had been pegged out.

THE QUESTION OF BLIND HOLES

It is not nearly as common an error to make blind holes as formerly. A blind tee shot may be forgiven, or a full shot to the green on a seaside course, when the greens can usually be located accurately by the position of the surrounding hummocks, but an approach shot should never be blind, as this prevents an expert player, except by a fluke, from placing his approach so near the hole that he gets down in one putt.

Blind holes on an inland course where there are no surrounding sandhills to locate the green should never be permitted, but an even more annoying form of blindness is that which is so frequent on inland courses—that is, when the flag is visible but the surface of the green cannot be seen. On a green of this description no one can possibly tell whether the flag is at the back, middle, or front of the green, and it is particularly aggravating to play your shot expecting to find it dead, and to discover that your ball is at least twenty yards short.

On a seaside course there may be a certain amount of pleasurable excitement in running up to the top of a hillock in the hope of seeing your ball near the flag, but this is a kind of thing one gets rather tired of as one grows older.

IMPORTANCE OF BEAUTY

Another common erroneous idea is that beauty does not matter on a golf course. One often hears players say that they don't care a " tinker's cuss " about their surroundings: what they want is good golf.

One of the best-known writers on golf has recently been jeering at golf architects for attempting to make beautiful bunkers. If he prefers ugly bunkers, ugly greens, and ugly surroundings generally he is welcome to them, but I don't think for an instant that he believes what he is writing about, for at the same time he talks about the beauties of natural courses. The chief object of every golf architect or green-keeper worth his salt is to imitate the beauties of nature so closely as to make his work indistinguishable from nature itself.

I haven't the smallest hesitation in saying that beauty means a great deal on a golf course; even the man who emphatically states he does not care a hang for beauty is subconsciously influenced by his surroundings. A beautiful hole not only appeals to the short handicap player but also to the long, and there are few first-rate holes which are not at the same time, either in the grandeur of their undulations and hazards, or the character of their surroundings, beautiful holes.

It is not suggested that we should all play round the links after the manner of the curate playing with the deaf old Scotsman.

The curate was audibly expressing his admiration of the scenery, the greens, and things in general, until they finally arrived at a green surrounded by a rookery. The curate remarked, "Isn't it delightful to hear the rooks?" The deaf old Scotsman said, " What's that ? " The curate again remarked, " Isn't it delightful to hear the rooks ? " The old Scotsman replied, " I can't hear a word you're saying for those damned crows."

The finest courses in existence are natural ones. Such courses as St. Andrews, and the championship courses generally, are admitted to provide a fine test of golf. It is by virtue of their natural formation that they do so. The beauty of gold courses has suffered in the past from the creations of ugly and unimaginative design. Square, flat greens and geometrical bunkers have not only been an eyesore upon the whole landscape, but have detracted from the infinite variety of play which is the heritage of the game.

My reputation in the past has been based on the fact that I have endeavoured to conserve existing natural features, and where these are lacking to create formations in the spirit of nature herself.

In other words, while always keeping uppermost the provision of a splendid test of golf, I have striven to achieve beauty.

It may at first appear unreasonable that the question of æsthetics should enter into golf-course design; however, on deeper analysis, it becomes clear that the great courses, and in detail all the famous holes and greens, are fascinating to the golfer by reason of their shape, their situation, and the character of their modelling. When these elements obey the fundamental laws of balance, of harmony, and fine proportion they give rise to what we call beauty. This excellence of design is more felt than fully realised by the player, but nevertheless it is constantly exercising a subconscious influence upon him, and in course of time he grows to admire such a course as all works of beauty are eventually felt and admired.

THE REAL OBJECT OF THE HAZARD

Most of the remaining principles depend on the proper disposition of hazards, and I have a rather wider definition of hazards than is given by the rules of Golf Committee. As a minor kind of hazard undulating ground, hummocks, hollows, etc., might be included.

Most golfers have an entirely erroneous view of the real object of hazards. The majority of them simply look upon hazards as a means of punishing a bad shot, when their real object is to make the game interesting. The attitude of the ordinary golfer towards hazards may be illustrated by the following tale which I have frequently told before, but which will bear repeating :

A player visiting a Scotch course asked his caddie what the members thought of a stream which was winding in and out between several of the holes. The caddie replied, " Weel, we've got an old Scotch major here. When he gets it ower he says, ' Weel ower the bonnie wee burn, ma laddie ' ; but when he gets in he says, ' Pick ma ball oot o' that domned sewer.' "

The writer was recently playing with his brother, who was home on leave from abroad. He was clearly enjoying his game, but at Alwoodley we have one solitary pond into which he topped three balls. On arriving at the club-house he was asked how he liked the course; he simply remarked, " There were too many ruddy ponds about."

It is much too large a subject to go into the question of the placing of hazards, but I would like to emphasise a fundamental principle. It is that, as already pointed out, no hazard is unfair wherever it is placed.

A hazard placed in the exact position

The fifteenth hole on the City of Newcastle course: constructed on flat, featureless clay land.

where a player would naturally go is frequently the most interesting situation, as then a special effort is needed to get over or avoid it.

GIVING THE PLAYER THRILLS

One of the objects in placing hazards is to give the players as much pleasurable excitement as possible. On many inland courses there is not a thrill on the whole round, and yet on some of the championship courses one rarely takes a club out of the bag without having an interesting shot to play. This particularly applies to the old course at St. Andrews, and is one of the reasons why it always retains its popularity with all classes of players. It is quite true that even this course is condemned by some, but this may be due to the fact that they have not brains enough, or have not played on it long enough, to appreciate its many virtues.

There are some leading players who

honestly dislike the dramatic element in golf. They hate anything that is likely to interfere with a constant succession of threes and fours. They look upon everything in the "card and pencil" spirit. The average club member on the other hand is a keen sportsman, he looks upon golf in the "spirit of adventure," and that is why St. Andrews and courses modelled on similar ideals appeal to him.

No one would pretend that the old course at St. Andrews is perfect: it has its disadvantages, particularly in the absence of long carries from the tee, and in its blind bunkers, but no links in the world grows upon all classes of players in the same manner. The longer one plays there the keener one gets, and this is a much truer test of a good course than one which pleases at first and is boring later on.

A good golf course is like good music or good anything else; it is not necessarily a course which appeals the first time one plays over it, but one which grows on the player the more frequently he visits it.

St. Andrews is a standing example of the possibility of making a course which is pleasurable to all classes of golfers, not only to the thirty handicap players, but to the plus fourteen man, if there ever was or will be such a person.

It is an interesting fact that few hazards are of any interest which are out of what is known among medical men as the direct field of vision. This does not extend much farther than ten to twenty yards on either side of the direct line to the hole. Hazards placed outside this limit are usually of little interest, but simply act as a source of irritation.

Hazards should be placed with an object, and none should be made which has not some influence on the line of play to the hole.

TOO MANY BUNKERS

On many courses there are far too many bunkers: the sides of the fairways are riddled with them, and many of these courses would be equally interesting if half of the bunkers were turfed over as grassy hollows.

It is often possible to make a hole sufficiently interesting with one or two bunkers at the most. For example:

It is obvious from the diagram that the green-guarding bunker B has a considerable influence on the line of play to the hole.

The longer the carry a player achieves over the stream the easier his second shot becomes.

If it were not for this bunker not only the approach but the tee shot would be uninteresting, as there would be no object in essaying the long carry over the stream.

Many poor golf courses are made in

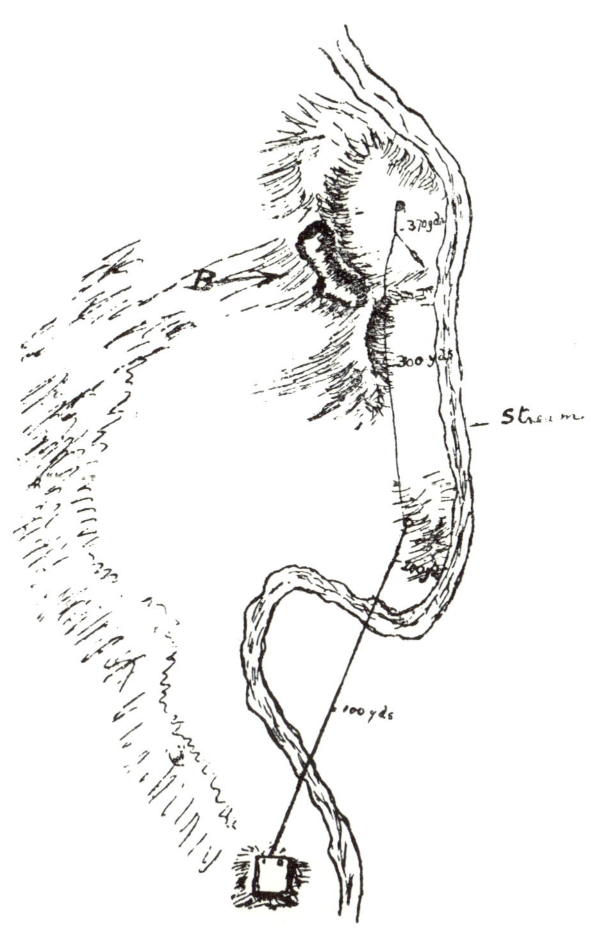

DIAGRAM OF HOLE OF 370 YARDS, ILLUSTRATING THE VALUE OF ONE BUNKER, B. Any additional bunker for the tee shot or across the approach to the green would materially lessen the interest of the hole. The moral is "Few bunkers placed in interesting positions!"

a futile attempt to eliminate the element of luck. You can no more eliminate luck in golf than in cricket, and in neither case is it possible to punish every bad shot. If you succeeded you would only make both games uninteresting.

There are many points of resemblance between cricket and golf: the fielders in cricket correspond to the hazards at golf. The fielders are placed in the positions where the majority of shots go, and it should obviously be easier with a stationary ball to avoid the hazards than to avoid the fielders at cricket.

In both games it is only a proportion of bad shots that get punished, but notwithstanding this the man who is playing the best game almost invariably comes out on top.

It is an important thing in golf to make holes look much more difficult than they really are. People get more pleasure in doing a hole which looks almost impossible, and yet is not so difficult as it appears.

In this connection it may be pointed out that rough grass is of little interest as a hazard. It is frequently much more difficult than a fearsome-looking bunker or belt of whins or rushes, but it causes considerable annoyance in lost balls, and no one ever gets the same thrills in driving over a stretch of rough as over a fearsome-looking bunker, which in reality may not be so severe.

Narrow fairways bordered by long grass make bad golfers. They do so by destroying the harmony and continuity of the game, and in causing a stilted and cramped style by destroying all freedom of play.

There is no defined line between the fairways in the great schools of golf like St. Andrews or Hoylake.

It is a common error to cut the rough in straight lines. It should be cut in irregular, natural-looking curves. The fairways should gradually widen out where a long drive goes; in this way a long driver is given a little more latitude in pulling and slicing.

Moreover irregular curves assist a player in locating the exact position of a ball which has left the fairway and entered the rough.

GLORIFIED MOLE-HILLS

Hummocks and hollows should be made of all sorts of different shapes and sizes, and should have a natural appearance, with plenty of slope at the bottom like large waves. Most of the hummocks and hollows should be made so smooth that the mowing machine can be used over them. The glorified mole-hills one sees on many courses should be avoided.

Bunkers on an inland course should, as a rule, be made in the opposite way to what is customary. At the present time

THE ARTIFICIAL HUMMOCKS GUARDING THE FIFTH GREEN AT ALWOODLEY : approximate cost, £8.

The best way of combining sand and hummocks, with the sand on he slope of the hazard above the ground level.

49]

most bunkers have the hollows sanded and the banks turfed. It is suggested that you get a much more natural appearance if the hollows are partly turfed over and the hummocks sanded, as in the photographs in these pages. This has the following advantages: the appearance is much more like a seaside course; the sand being above the level of the ground, always remains dry. The contrast between white or yellow sand and the grass helps one to judge distances much more accurately, and enables the ball to be found more easily, and the great disadvantage and expense of scything the long grass on the hummocks to prevent lost balls is done away with.

Ordinary bunkers are, as a rule, made in quite the wrong way. The face is usually too upright and the ball gets into an unplayable position under the face. The bottom of the bank of a bunker should have a considerable slope, so that a ball always rolls to the middle; the top of a bunker may, as it usually does in nature, be made to overhang a little so as to prevent a topped ball running through it.

Experience gained in the imitation of natural slopes in bunker-making was ultimately responsible for saving tens of thousands of pounds in revetting material in the great war.

Trenches with the sides made like a bank of a stream with a considerable slope at the bottom remained standing without any revetting material.

Before this principle was pointed out soldiers invariably dug their trenches with a slope at the top, and as they got farther down the sides became more vertical and sometimes were even undercut. A trench of this kind invariably fell in, whereas those made vertical at the top with the slope at the bottom did not do so.

Hazards are usually placed too far

away from the greens they are intended to guard; they should be placed immediately on the edge of the greens, and then (particularly if they are in the form of smooth hillocks and hollows) the player who is wide of them has an extremely difficult pitch, and is frequently worse off than the man who is in them.

A bunker eating into a green is by far the most equitable way of giving a golfer full advantage for accurate play. It not only penalises the man who is in it, but every one who is wide of it. For example, a player who is in the road bunker at the seventeenth at St. Andrews may with a good dunch shot get out and lie dead, but few can pitch over it so accurately that they do so. A bunker, similarly placed to the road bunker, may be made to accentuate this distinction; it may be constructed with so much slope that on occasions it can be putted out of.

Hummocks on the edge of greens are

often constructed so that they assist the man who has opened up the hole correctly ; they act as a hazard only to those who have failed to do this.

Perhaps the most serious mistake made by a golf committee is the fallacy that they will save money by neglecting to obtain expert advice in regard to fresh construction work.

Except where the course has been designed and the construction work supervised by the modern golf architect, there is hardly a golf club of any size which has not frittered away hundreds of pounds in doing bad work, all for the want of the best advice in the first instance.

There can be little doubt that the poorer the club the more important it is for it not to waste its small funds in doing the wrong kind of work, but to get the best possible advice from its inception.

THE SEVENTEENTH GREEN AT HARROGATE: APPROXIMATE COST £180: an entirely artificial plateau green constructed on flat land. The comparatively heavy cost is due to the character of the subsoil—heavy clay.

THE COURSE FOR THE BEGINNER

I notice a well-known club, in forming a golf course, state that the committee have decided to lay it out themselves, as they are afraid of a golf architect making it too difficult for the average player. Now this is precisely what the modern golf architect does not do; he in particular adopts a most sympathetic attitude to the beginner and long handicap player, but at the same time attempts to make the course interesting to all sorts and conditions of players. It is characteristic of the modern architect that he always leaves a broad and pleasurable road that leads to destruction—that is, sixes and sevens on the card of the long handicap player—but a straight and narrow path which leads to salvation—that is, threes and fours for the plus man.

The writer has just returned from a

most delightful sand-dune country which he chose for his holiday in great part owing to the fact that he had seen it before and had also seen Mr. Colt's plan for the constructing of what should have been the finest eighteen-hole course in England.

On arrival he found the secretary or the committee had, through motives of false economy, refrained from getting Mr. Colt to supervise the work and had done it themselves. The outcome was an expenditure of three or four times as much money as Mr. Colt would have needed, the destruction of many of the beautiful natural undulations and features which were the making of Mr. Colt's scheme, the conversion of magnificent visible greens into semi-blind ones, banked up like croquet lawns, and a complete absence of turf owing to wrong treatment, and alterations in the placing of the tees, bunkers, and greens, and a total disregard of the beginner and the long handicap player. On a seaside course in particular little construction work is necessary ; the important thing is to make the fullest possible use of existing features. £500 in labour expended under expert supervision is better than £10,000 injudiciously expended.

Surely in the case of a golf club it is more important to have an architect for the course, and any new work on the course, than for the club-house. Much greater mistakes are made in constructing the former than in building the latter.

One can readily imagine what would be the ultimate result of a course laid out by an average committee composed of scratch, three, four, and eight handicap men. They are, most of them (probably subconsciously), prejudiced against any hazard being constructed which they are likely to get into themselves, but they are all unanimous in thinking that the poor devil with a twenty-four handicap should be left out of consideration altogether. The final result is neither fish, flesh, fowl, nor even good red herring.

THE QUALIFICATIONS OF THE EXPERT

The expert in golf architecture has to be intimately conversant with the theory of playing the game, but this has no connection with the physical skill in playing it. An ideal golf expert should not only have a knowledge of botany, geology, and particularly agricultural chemistry, but should also have what might be termed an artistic temperament and vivid imagination. We all know that there is nothing so fatal in playing golf as to have a vivid imagination, but this and a sufficient knowledge of psychology to enable one to determine what is likely to give the greatest pleasure to the greatest number are eminently desirable in a golf architect. The training of the expert should be mental, not physical.

My last principle is one which particularly affects the green-keeper:—the course should be perfect all the year round.

It is quite a prevalent idea that courses on a clay subsoil can never be made into good winter links. It does not matter so much as might be expected, what the subsoil is like, provided it is well drained and the turf on the top is of the right texture. Muddy courses are entirely due to insufficient drainage, worms, and the wrong kind of turf.

Worms can be got rid of and the right kind of turf encouraged by adopting modern methods of green-keeping. Many examples of what can be done in converting really bad winter courses into good ones can be seen in the North. Surface drainage, such as mole draining, gets rid of worms by making the land so dry that they cannot work.

SOME HINTS ON GREEN TREATMENT

A common mistake in green-keeping is to imagine that because one form of treatment benefits one course that it will necessarily benefit another.

The green-keeper should have sufficient knowledge of chemistry and botany to be able to tell exactly what form of treatment is most likely to benefit his greens.

For example, the ordinary artificial manure sold by some seeds merchants for golf courses consists of a mixture of three parts of superphosphate of lime, one part each sulphate of ammonia and sulphate of potash, and one-tenth part of sulphate of iron. If no weeds are present, the sulphate of iron may be omitted from the mixture; if daisies are present, the sulphate of ammonia should be increased; if clover is present, the potash and lime should be lessened in quantity; if the turf is sour, or if sorrel is present, the sulphate of ammonia should be lessened, and lime used as a separate dressing.

Farmyard manure should not, as a rule, be used as a surface dressing on golf courses: it is much too likely to encourage weeds and worms.

Something of the nature of Peruvian guano, fish guano, meat guano, malt culms, or dried blood, together with artificials, should be used in its place. If humus is necessary, it may be added in the form of peat moss litter, minced seaweed, etc., and the box should seldom be used on the mowing machines.

It must be borne in mind that the turf required on a golf course is entirely different to that required from a farming point of view.

It is now an absolutely exploded fallacy that worms are of any use on a golf course; they should be got rid of by the use of charcoal obtained from steel furnaces: ordinary wood charcoal is almost useless. Charcoal in this form acts mechanically, owing to the small sharp pieces of steel attached to it: it scratches the worms and prevents them getting through.

Worm-killers, especially those consisting of Mowrah Meal, are of great value in destroying worms.

It is a mistake to consider that worm-killers, unless mixed with an artificial manure, have any manurial value. The green-keeper will tell you that after the application the grass has come up much greener. That is due to the fact that the worms are no longer discolouring it by crawling over it with their slimy bodies.

THE MOWING OF GREENS

A common mistake is not to mow greens during the winter months. I have not the slightest doubt that mowing greens during the winter months is beneficial to them : it keeps the grass from becoming coarse.

On those Scotch courses where the greens are so good all through the winter, are not the rabbits mowing the greens all through the winter months ?

Are the knives of the mowing machine any more likely to do the grass harm than the teeth of the rabbits ?

It is a common mistake in sowing a green not to use a sufficient quantity of seed. The ground should always be thoroughly prepared and manured according to the chemical composition of the soil ; then as much as five or six bushels of seed per green can be sown to advantage.

Mixtures of grass seeds may be sold consisting of a considerable proportion of seeds which do not germinate, and are not likely to do so, on ordinary soils. Unscrupulous seeds merchants may undercut the more honest ones in this way. Three bushels of the best seeds will go further than six containing a large proportion of varieties which are not likely to germinate.

In concluding this chapter on General Principles, it may be pointed out that, although many of these ideas may appear revolutionary, the reader may be assured that their success under varying conditions has been proved in practice.

GRANGE-OVER-SANDS: the site of one of the greens on the rocks near the boundary of the course—work just beginning.

GRANGE-OVER-SANDS: ready for turfing—a green constructed on rocks.

63]

CHAPTER II

SOME FURTHER SUGGESTIONS

It cannot be too frequently emphasised that in starting a new course or reconstructing an old one it is of the utmost importance that the committee should have a scheme before them of a definite and final nature. It would be sound finance for the majority of golf clubs to pay the expenses of the Green Committee for the purpose of visiting good examples of construction work on other courses.

They should not of necessity visit courses where the leading open competitions are held, as many of the very best clubs rarely offer their courses for competitions.

They should be guided in their choice of architect by a course constructed out of indifferent material, and not by one constructed out of magnificent natural golfing land.

They should take into consideration the cost, the popularity with all classes of players, and the finality and permanency of the work.

Having decided on the architect and having passed the plan, it is as well to take steps to ensure that the construction work is done according to the ideas of the designer.

Experience of advising a hundred golf clubs has convinced the writer that the work can never be done properly except under occasional expert supervision. Work done without expert supervision is invariably bad.

The designer should not be tied down too closely to his original plan. Mature consideration and unexpected changes in the subsoil, etc., may make a modification in the plan necessary to save expense and get better results.

In a small book of this kind, it is impossible to go into the thousand and one details which make for economy in course construction, but some of these may be enumerated.

The chief items in the construction of a golf course are the following:

1. Carting.
2. Labour.
3. Drainage.
4. Seeding.
5. Turfing.
6. Manures.
7. Sand.

CARTING

The cost of carting can often be reduced to a minimum by using a little thought in the work. The stone from stone walls, rocks, the turf from turf walls, or soil taken out of excavations should never be carted away: they can always be used for raising a neighbouring green in the form of a plateau, or in making hummocks or large undulations indistinguishable from the natural ones which are so delightful on seaside courses. It is rarely necessary to cart soil from a distance for the purpose of making a hummock or a green. It is much more economical to remove a sufficient area of turf from and around the site of an intended hummock or green, and utilise the soil removed from the area around the hummock for this purpose. This is a double advantage. The surrounding ground is lowered as the hummock is raised, and makes the hummock appear higher, and at the same time it is made to merge imperceptibly into the surrounding hollow or hollows, and has a much more natural appearance. A hollow removed from the front of the green has the effect of making the green appear as if it were raised upon a plateau, and this is still further accentuated if the soil removed is also used to build up the green.

Similarly the green and the bunkers guarding it should all be made at the same time; the soil moved in making the bunkers can then be utilised in the formation of the green. It was in former years considered imprudent to construct bunkers until the experience of playing revealed the proper position, but since those days our knowledge of green-keeping has advanced. An expert can judge by the character of the grasses and the nature of the undulations the amount of run which the ball is likely to get, and this knowledge, combined with actual measurements, gives more information than it is possible to gain by playing. Perhaps the most important reason why the architect's scheme should be completed in the first instance is that bunkers are hardly ever placed in the right position afterwards. It is difficult to find a member of a Green Committee who is not subconsciously prejudiced against placing a bunker where he is likely to get trapped himself.

After carting there is usually a considerable amount of labour necessary to obliterate the tracks. Carting should, when possible, be done when the ground is hard, in dry weather or during frost. Carts should not be allowed to wander about all over the place, but should be made to keep in one track. It is often advisable to remove the turf previous to carting and relay it after the carting is finished. Carts can sometimes be replaced with advantage by sledges with flat-bottomed runners.

LABOUR AT LESS THAN PRE-WAR COST

By introducing labour-saving machinery we have recently been getting better results at less than pre-war cost. If work on a large scale is being done, the steam navvy

THE "SCRAPER" AT WORK ON WHEATLEY PARK COURSE, DONCASTER.

or grab might be tried for excavating and making hummocks, etc.; traction engines are useful in uprooting small trees, and larger ones can with advantage be blown up by dynamite. I recently used blasting charges for the purpose of assisting to make bunkers. An article in one of the Sheffield papers somewhat humorously stated that this was not the first occasion Dr. Mackenzie's bunkers had been "blasted."

Trolleys on rails are frequently used to save carting or wheeling barrows.

The two machines which are found of the greatest value in saving labour are the turf-cutting machine and the American scraper or scoop—the former made from designs by the writer. It will cut an acre of sods in an afternoon, and, moreover, cuts them of a more even thickness than by hand. This machine is worked by two horses like a plough. One or two clubs have condemned it without a fair trial, and on inquiry I have usually found that the weather was too dry, the grass too long, the blades had not been set properly, or that it had been used by a man who had had no previous experience in working one. It has been used by scores of clubs with a great deal of success. At Moortown we sodded over twenty acres of sour heath land with it. The cost of this amounted to little compared with sowing, as we were able to remove the sods from a neighbouring field. Sowing would have cost at least twice as much, as there were no signs of even a blade of grass on most of the land, and no sowing was likely to be successful without lime and manuring, and carting a tremendous quantity of soil so as to form a seed bed. The results have been infinitely better and quicker than sowing at the rate of even twelve bushels of the best grass seeds to the acre.

The scraper is worked by a horse or two

GRANGE-OVER-SANDS: the turf-cutting machine at work. The photograph shows the dead, flat, featureless character of the country before the work began.

Grange-over-Sands: sandhills constructed by means of the scraper on terrain originally perfectly flat.

horses, and is particularly useful for excavating light soil, but can even be used on heavy land if each layer is ploughed before the scraper is used. The scraper is shaped like a large shovel, the handles are raised, and the horse pulls and it digs into the ground until it is full; the handles are then depressed and the horse pulls it along to the required situation; it is then tipped up, and the horse returns for another load. One horse and two men by this means can do the work of a score of men working in the ordinary way with wheelbarrows. In making hollows and hummocks it has an additional advantage in that it gives them automatically a natural appearance, and at the same time the horse in climbing up to the top of the hump compresses the soil, and it does not sink so much afterwards.

The scraper has been used with considerable success at Castletown (Isle of

Man), Wheatley Park (Doncaster), and Grange-over-Sands, among other courses.

It is important in constructing a new or altering an old course to get the work done as quickly as possible: if the work is done gradually the sods lie about for some time and are sometimes ruined. Most of the work should be done during October and November, before the frosts commence: good methods of organisation should prevent men being unemployed during frost. If the greens, drains, and sites of bunkers are previously pared, and the sods allowed to lie, then even though frost sets in, the sods may be removed and a certain amount of excavation can still be proceeded with. Sand, soil, and manures may be carted, hedges stubbed up, and trees removed during frost.

DRAINAGE

It is advisable to drain golfing land much more thoroughly and efficiently than ordinary farm land, but, on the other hand, by exercising a little thought it can be done much more cheaply. For the purpose of golf it is not only unnecessary to drain as deeply as is customary for agricultural purposes, but it is much cheaper and more satisfactory to adopt a system of shallow drains.

On a golf course, there is never any necessity to make allowance for the possibility of subsoil ploughing; the drains can therefore be kept near the surface. The great thing to bear in mind in draining is that the water stratum must be tapped. On heavy clay land, it is absurd to put drains in the middle of the clay, unless the whole of the trench is filled with clinkers or other porous material, and this is needlessly expensive. Drains may at times be placed in a groove on the surface of the clay. On land of this description drains may often be placed with advantage at as shallow a depth as from

6 to 12 inches. It should be unnecessary to state that no effort should be spared to see that there is sufficient fall, and for the purpose of ensuring this it is often necessary to take the levels. Sufficient thought is rarely given to drainage. The site of the main drains and the whole scheme of drainage should be very carefully studied, and it is of special importance to take into consideration the nature of the subsoil and position of the water level. In peat, on the other hand, it is frequently advisable to drain below the peat, even if this extends to a depth of 6 feet or more. If this is impossible owing to lack of sufficient fall, wooden boards should be placed below the drains.

The cheapest method of draining is by a system of mole drainage. I have frequently used a mole drain worked by horses which was made from suggestions by Franks, the Moortown green-keeper, and myself. It is used as an attachment to the turf-cutting machine. By this method golf courses on clay land could be drained, previous to the war, at less than a pound per acre.

This mole drain works at the shallow depth of 6 inches, and is not applicable to agricultural land, as even horses galloping over the ground are sufficient to block the channel. It is, morcover, wonderfully satisfactory on golfing land, especially as supplementary to ordinary tile draining. Whenever the ground is sticky, or any casual water appears, the mole is run through and it becomes absolutely dry at once. This mole drain has a big advantage over the larger one, in that the cut made by the mole is so small that it does not interfere with the lie of the ball.

We have recently used a tractor instead of horses to pull the mole, and have found it a great advantage to do so. The use of the mole provides a solution for the problem of converting the muddiest of clay London courses into good winter links. Experience has proved that the effect lasts for fully ten years.

One of the most remarkable results of its use is that it gets rid of worms. This is probably owing to the fact that it makes the ground so dry that the worms can't work in it.

It also prevents the ground becoming baked during dry summer weather. This is a well-known effect of good drainage, although possibly an unexpected one to the uninitiated. It is largely due to the drainage preventing the ground becoming caked, and also to the encouragement of turf with a good bottom to it.

TURFING

The cheapest and best method of removing turf is by means of a turf-cutting machine. The thickness of the turf should vary according to the nature of the grasses and the character of the subsoil. As a general rule, turf for greens should be cut as thin as 1½ inches. This is particularly important if the turf contains many tap-rooted weeds; the roots of the weeds and many of the coarser grasses are then left behind in the cutting.

In the experience of the writer, it is frequently not a difficult matter to get excellent turf in the immediate neighbourhood of a golf course at an extremely cheap rate—a halfpenny a yard or under—and turf obtained from the immediate neighbourhood of the course is much more likely to be suitable than turf obtained elsewhere. The writer has known a golf club going to the expense of getting Silloth turf at 9*d.* a yard, the grasses of which would inevitably disappear and be replaced by those of its environment within a year or two, when much more suitable turf could be obtained from the next field at a cost of a farthing a yard.

It should be borne in mind that the most useless turf from a farming point of view is frequently the most valuable for golf. There are many other details which help to lessen the cost of turfing. In an old-established course, turf for new greens or for renovating old ones can frequently be obtained from the sides of a neighbouring fairway, the sods from which may be replaced by those removed from the site of the green.

There is usually a well-trodden path extending from every tee to the nearest fairway. There is no turf so useful for renovating an old or making a new tee as that obtained from a firm path of this kind. The sods removed should be replaced by others, and they in turn get hard and firm.

An important question is the use of manures in turfing. Stable or farmyard manure should almost invariably be placed under the sods: the amount should vary according to the turf and soil. Five loads per green is an average, and on undulating greens the manure should be placed under the raised portions only. The hollows will look after themselves. Manure does more harm than good if dug deeply in: it should be forked in immediately under the sods, and the roots of the finer grasses feed on it at once. If dug in deeply, the coarser grasses are encouraged at the expense of the finer.

On wormy inland courses considerable expense in worm-killers can frequently be saved by placing a few loads of coke breeze under the sods.

Although the best time to turf is in the late autumn and winter months, sods can, if necessity arises, be laid in certain localities as late as June.

If hot dry weather arrives, the newly laid sods should be covered with cut grass during the day, and in the evening the grass should be removed so that the dews help to keep the ground moist.

SEEDING

The writer has known of several instances where ground has been sown, and the result has been so unsatisfactory that after a year or two the land had to be ploughed up and resown.

It is much more economical in the long run to do the thing thoroughly. Mistakes are most frequently made in sowing with the wrong seeds—in not preparing the ground thoroughly beforehand, and in sowing at the wrong time of year.

It is most important that a mixture should be chosen containing a goodly proportion of seeds corresponding to the prevailing grasses of the immediate neighbourhood, and seeds should always be obtained from a seeds merchant who is not afraid of telling you the exact composition of his mixture. Some seeds merchants sell mixtures which are not so valuable for golfing turf as they appear—it is not the best kind of grass which germinates too quickly. Finer turf usually results from a mixture which comes up more slowly but is of a more permanent character. If seeding is necessary, it is frequently advisable to sow with much larger quantity of seed than is customary.

It is of the utmost importance to prepare the land thoroughly before sowing. The ground should be well drained, the land well limed when necessary, and fifteen loads to the acre of well-rotted stable manure incorporated with the soil or a mixture of artificial manure in its stead.

After sowing see that the birds are scared away by one of the numerous devices suggested for the purpose.

MANURES

It is surprising how much money can be saved in manures by the help of science and a sufficient knowledge of chemistry to enable you to judge which are the cheapest and most valuable manures suitable for the soil of the locality with which you have to deal.

It is often advisable to make a point of studying the by-products of the different industries in the district, as it is obvious that if a suitable manure for the soil can be obtained on the spot, it is obtained cheaper than by rail or cart from a distance. Fish or meat guano, basic slag, malt dust, sulphate of ammonia, chalk, the refuse from leather, cloth, and shoddy factories, seed crushing mills, seaweed, manure extracted from town sewage works, peat moss litter, etc., are all of value under different circumstances.

Basic slag can sometimes be obtained from a neighbouring steel works, sulphate of ammonia from a gas works, chalk from a neighbouring chalk pit, or seaweed from the seashore. Manures should be used with a considerable amount of discretion and only in small quantities at a time. I have known a considerable amount of damage done by the unintelligent use of artificials. For example, artificials are of the greatest possible value for golfing turf, but they should always be used in small quantities but frequently, and should be well diluted with soil or sand, and only used during moist weather. A mixture, consisting of superphosphate of lime, sulphate of ammonia, and sulphate of potash, supplies most of the feeding material that is necessary for golf, and the experiments at Rothamstead conclusively prove that the character of the grasses can be completely altered by varying the proportion of the different constituents of this mixture.

Sulphate of ammonia is the most valuable of the constituents of this mixture, but I have known of several greens (including even St. Andrews) temporarily ruined by using sulphate of ammonia injudiciously. It should never be put on a green undiluted, as, like most artificials, it has a great affinity for water, and in dry weather absorbs the water from the grasses and burns them up. It also should never be used if the land is the least bit sour, as it simply increases this sourness.

A green-keeper should attempt to get a sufficient knowledge of botany and chemistry to know by the character of the herbage of his greens the kind and the amount of manure that is required. Green-keepers sometimes think that if they use twice the usual quantity of a manure, it will have double the effect; the exact contrary is the case, as the green may be ruined entirely.

The most important manure of all is cut grass. If the cut grass is always left on the greens and fairways, very little manuring is necessary. On the other hand, if the grass is constantly removed year after year (unless a considerable amount of manure is added to take its place), the turf becomes impoverished and full of weeds. One of the unexpected results of leaving the grass on is that less mowing is necessary. This is probably due to the fact that the growth goes into the roots and not into the leaves. Mowing without the box on is of special importance on sandy or seaside courses.

SAND

Sand is often an expensive item on an inland course. It is surprising how frequently a good class of sand is found in pockets on a course or in the immediate neighbourhood. A knowledge of geology and botany will enable you to foretell where sand is likely to be found.

On several occasions on visiting a course I have been told that there was no sand in the district, and have been able to find some by noting the character of the trees, grasses, etc. Sand may be economised by the method in which bunkers are made. It will be noticed in the photographs reproduced that most of the hollows have been turfed, but have been formed in such a way that a ball gravitates towards the sand, which is thrown up against the face. Bunkers of this description have a much more natural appearance, and the amount of sand needed is also considerably less than usual.

By far the most important of all the foregoing suggestions is the ultimate economy of making it as reasonably certain as possible that any work done is of a permanent character and has not ultimately to be done over again. There are few committees of golf clubs who attach sufficient importance to expert advice. I suppose this is partly due to the fact that they themselves would sooner have the work done badly and have the

A BUNKER ON THE FULFORD COURSE, ARTIFICIALLY CONSTRUCTED ON FLAT LAND AT A COST OF £3.

fun of doing it than see any one else do it for them. In the nature of things a course can only be constructed by an individual: "Too many cooks spoil the broth" is a proverb which is more applicable in the case of golf courses than in anything else.

I personally am a strong believer in encouraging the individuality of the greenkeeper, and not interfering with, but rather encouraging, his original ideas, unless they are in opposition to sound fundamental principles.

CHAPTER III

IDEAL HOLES

THERE are few problems more difficult to solve than the problem of what exactly constitutes an ideal hole. The ideal hole is surely one that affords the greatest pleasure to the greatest number, gives the fullest advantage for accurate play, stimulates players to improve their game, and never becomes monotonous.

The real practical test is its popularity, and here again we are up against another difficulty. Does the average player really know what he likes himself? One often hears the same player expressing totally divergent opinions about the same hole. When he plays it successfully, it is everything that is good, and when unsuccessful it is everything that is bad. It frequently happens that the best holes give rise to the most bitter controversy. It is largely a question of the spirit in which the problem is approached. Does the player look upon it from the "card and pencil" point of view and condemn anything that has disturbed his steady series of threes and fours, or does he approach the question in the "spirit of adventure" of the true sportsman ?

There are well-known players who invariably condemn any hole they have taken over six for, and if by any chance they ever reach double figures, words fail them to describe in adequate language what they think of that particular hole.

It does not by any means follow that when a player condemns a hole in particularly vigorous language he really dislikes it. It may be a source of pleasure to his subconscious mind. Although condemning it, he may be longing to play it again so as to conquer its difficulties.

Who is to judge what is an ideal hole? Is it one of our leading players, or any golfer who simply looks upon it from his own point of view? I have known of an open champion expressing his opinion that a certain course was superior to any in Britain. As far as this particular course is concerned, it is generally admitted by amateurs that, although the turf and natural advantages were excellent, it had not a single hole of any real merit. The local committee were also of opinion that it was monotonous and lacking in real interest, and had decided to have it entirely remodelled, before this world renowned open champion persuaded them to change their minds by expressing such strong views in its favour.

There are, unfortunately, many leading players who wish a course to be designed so that it will favour their own play and will not even punish their indifferent shots, but will put any one below their particular standard out of the running altogether.

There are many leading players who condemn the strategic aspect of golf. They only see one line to the hole, and that is usually the direct one. They cannot see why they should, as in dog-legged holes, be ever compelled to play to one or other side of the direct line. A bunker in the direct line at the distance of their long drives is invariably condemned by them, because they do not realise that the correct line is to one or other side of it. Why should not even an open champion occasionally have a shot that the long handicap man is frequently compelled to play?

Should a course or hole be ideal from a medal or match-playing point of view? If it is necessary to draw any distinction between the two, there can be little doubt that match play should always have prior claim. Nine out of ten games on most good courses are played in matches and not for medals. The true test of a hole is, then, its value in match play.

The majority of golfers are agreed, I think, that an ideal hole should be a difficult one. It is true there are some who would have it difficult for every one except themselves. These, who usually belong to the pot-hunting fraternity, may be left out of consideration. It is the successful negotiation of difficulties, or apparent ones, which gives rise to pleasurable excitement and makes a hole interesting.

What kind of difficulties make interesting golf?

We can, I think, eliminate difficulties consisting of long grass, narrow fairways, and small greens, because of the annoyance and irritation caused by searching for lost balls, the disturbance of the harmony and continuity of theg ame, the consequent loss of freedom of swing, and the production of bad players.

We can also eliminate blind greens, blind bunkers, and blind approaches. The greater the experience the writer has of designing golf courses, the more certain he is that blindness of all kinds should be avoided. The only form of blindness that should ever be permitted is the full shot up to a green whose position is accurately located by surrounding sand-hills. Even in a hole of this kind, it is not the blindness that is interesting, but the visibility of the surrounding sand-hills. At the Maiden hole at Sandwich, it was the grandeur and the impressiveness of the Maiden that made it a good hole, and not the blindness of the green.

The difficulties that make a hole really interesting are usually those in which a great advantage can be gained in successfully accomplishing heroic carries over hazards of an impressive appearance, or in taking great risks in placing a shot so as to gain a big advantage for the next. Successfully carrying or skirting a bunker of an alarming or impressive appearance is always a source of satisfaction to the golfer, and yet it is hazards of this description which so often give rise to criticism by the unsuccessful player. At first sight he looks upon it as grossly unfair that, of two shots within a few inches of each other, the one should be hopelessly buried in a bunker and the other should be in an ideal position.

However, on further consideration he will realise that, as in dog-legged holes, this is the chief characteristic of all good holes.

Holes of this description not only cater for great judgment, but great skill: a man who has such confidence that he can place his ball within a few feet of his objective gains a big advantage over a faint-hearted opponent who dare not take similar risks. On a course, with

The second hole at Headingley—cost £40. Hummock and bunkers entirely artificial: a two-shot dog-legged hole; the photo is taken along the line of the second shot.

holes of this kind, match play becomes of intense interest.

In a perfect hole the surface of not only the green, but the approach to it, should be visible. It is difficult, or even impossible, to judge an approach accurately unless the ground which the ball pitches on can be seen. It also gives great pleasure (or sometimes pain) to see the result of one's shot.

In an ideal hole, the turf should be as perfect as possible and the approaches should have the same consistency as the greens, but it is by no means advisable to avoid entirely bad lies or irregular stances. There is not only much skill required, but an improvement of one's game results in occasionally having to play out of a cupped lie, or from an uneven stance. There are few things more monotonous than always playing from a dead flat fairway.

In an ideal long hole, there should not

only be a big advantage from successfully negotiating a long carry for the tee shot, but the longer the drive, the greater the advantage should be. A shorter driver should also, by extreme accuracy, be able to gain an advantage over a long hitting but less accurate opponent.

An ideal hole should provide an infinite variety of shots according to the varying positions of the tee, the situation of the flag, the direction and strength of the wind, etc. It should also at times give full advantage for the voluntary pull or slice, one of the most finished shots in golf, and one that few champions are able to carry out with any great degree of accuracy.

Should an ideal hole be ideal for the plus, scratch, or long handicap player? As players of all handicaps play golf, a hole should as far as possible be ideal for all classes. There are many famous holes, such as the Cardinal, which are by no means ideal, as in an ideal hole there should always be an alternative route open to the weaker player.

Are there any ideal holes in existence at the present moment?

I think the eleventh (the short hole coming in at St. Andrews) may be considered so. Under certain conditions, it is extremely difficult for even the best player that ever breathed, especially if he is attempting to get a two, but at the same time an inferior player may get a four if he plays his own game exceptionally well. It has been suggested that the mere fact that it is possible to putt the whole length is an objection to it. No doubt the timid golfer can play the hole in this way, but he will lose strokes by avoiding risks. Even if an expert putter holes out in four strokes once in three times, he can consider himself lucky. I do not know of a solitary example of a player achieving success in an important match by this means. If a cross bunker were constructed at this hole, it would become appreciably diminished in interest in consequence. The narrow entrance and the subtle slopes have all the advantages of a cross bunker without making it impossible for the long handicap man. These contentions are borne out by those attempts that have been made to copy and improve on the hole by a cross bunker.

There are few, if any, other ideal short holes in existence. The seventh and fourteenth on the Eden Course at St. Andrews are remarkably fine holes, especially as they have to a great extent been artificially created. At the present moment the gorse in places is somewhat near both greens, but this can easily be rectified, and the architect, Mr. H. S. Colt, was wise in not removing too many whins in the first instance, as, if once removed, they cannot be replaced.

THE EIGHTH GREEN AT MOORTOWN: 170 yards, entirely artificial.

Another good example is the eighth at Moortown (formerly seventeenth, or, as it is known locally, Gibraltar). Its length is 170 yards, and it has been entirely artificially created at the small cost of £35.

The green has been constructed on a slight slope. The soil has been removed from the lower portion of the slope to make the bunkers and to bank up the green. The natural slope has been retained at the entrance to the green, and, like the eleventh at St. Andrews, it is these subtle slopes which lead a ball which has not been correctly hit, into the adjacent bunkers, and in reality have very much the same effect as a cross bunker without the hardship to the long handicap player.

The hole also shares with the eleventh at St. Andrews the necessity for an infinite variety of shots according to varying conditions of wind, position of flag, etc. One day it is a comparatively easy pitch with a mashie, normally it is a straight iron shot, sometimes a full shot with a trace of pull is required, and, again, it is necessary to slice so that one's ball is held up against the slope of the hill.

The green is delightfully picturesque. It is extremely visible against a background of fir trees—it stands up and looks at you.

The contrast between the vivid green of the grass, the dark green of the firs, the whiteness of the sand, the purple heather, and a vivid background of rhododendrons, combined with the natural appearance and extreme boldness of the contours, gives one a picture probably unsurpassed by anything of a similar kind in nature.

It is not only a delightful hole to see, which at any rate appeals subconsciously to the dullest of minds, but it is equally delightful to play. It is less difficult than it appears. You feel you are taking your

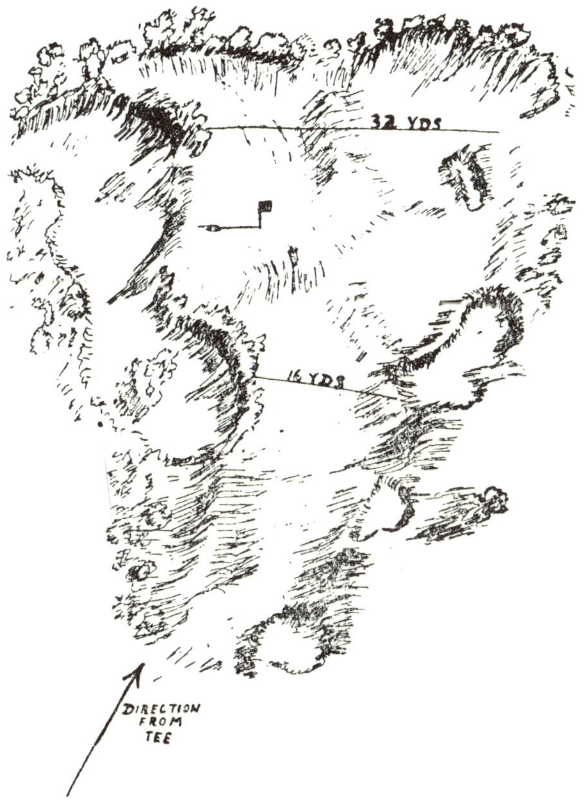

EIGHTH HOLE, "GIBRALTAR," MOORTOWN GOLF COURSE.

life in your hands, and it therefore appeals, as Mr. Bernard Darwin says, to the "spirit of adventure"—yet a well-played shot always gets its due reward.

There are few, if any, ideal two- or three-shot holes in existence. Some of those coming in at St. Andrews are almost, but not quite, perfect.

The sixteenth (Corner of the Dyke) hole at St. Andrews is almost ideal for its length (338 yards). It was a particularly good hole at the time of the guttie ball, and is so to-day for a short driver, like the writer.

As in the majority of good holes, it is the subtlety of the slopes that makes it so.

The green is tilted up slightly from right to left, and it would be a better hole still if the inclination were greater. It is also guarded by Grant's and the Wig Bunkers on the left-hand side, so that the approach from the right is

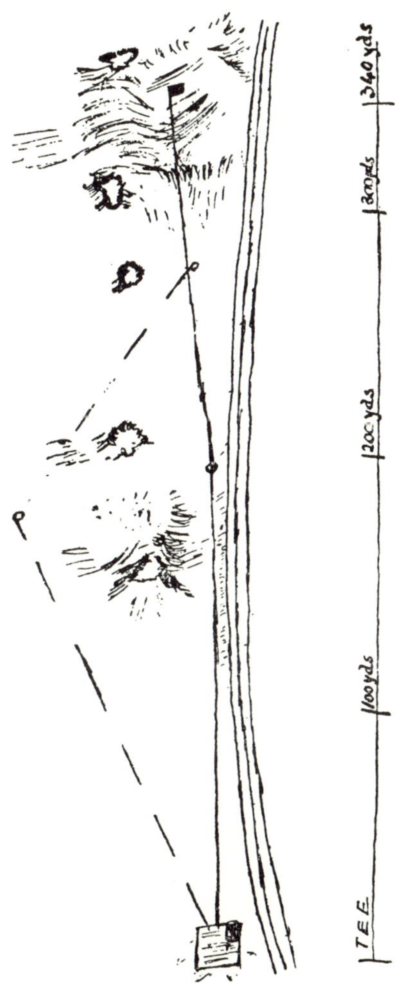

THE SIXTEENTH HOLE AT ST. ANDREWS.

easy, as all the slopes assist the players, and the approach from the left is exceedingly difficult.

The point about the hole is that it is so difficult to get into the best position to approach the green, because of the proximity of the Principal's Nose Bunker to the railway, and the difficulty of placing one's tee shot in such a small space with all the slopes leading to the bunker. On the other hand, there is a perfectly easy route free from all risk to the left of the Principal's Nose, but the player in all probability loses a stroke by taking it.

The fourteenth and seventeenth holes at St. Andrews are excellent holes, full of dramatic incident in match play.

The fourteenth hole is probably the best hole of its length in existence. Here, again, the hole is made by the slope of the green. There is a most marked tilt up from left to right, so much so that it is impossible to approach near the hole from the right. It is slopes of this kind which are so often overlooked in designing a golf course, and it is one of the most difficult things imaginable to construct them really well; but it is subtleties of this nature which make all the difference between a good course and a bad one.

At the fourteenth hole at St. Andrews this tilt of the green has a considerable influence on the tee shot 530 yards away. Some years ago there were four of us playing four ball matches nearly every day for a month. We, according to our own judgment, attempted to play this hole in four different ways. A played his tee shot well away to the left of the Beardies on to the low ground below the Elysian Fields, so as to place his second in a favourable position for his approach. B, who was a long driver, attempted to carry the Beardies with his drive, Hell with his second, and run up his third.

C, who was a short but fairly accurate hitter, attempted to pinch the Beardies as near as he dare, and then played his second well away to the left, so as to play against the slope of the green for his third. D took what was apparently the straightforward route along the large broad plateau of the Elysian Fields, and eventually landed in Hell or Perdition every time: he invariably lost the hole.

This hole is very nearly ideal, but would be better still if the lie of the land were such that the Beardies, the Crescent, the Kitchen, and Hell Bunkers were visible and impressive looking. If these bunkers only looked as terrifying and formidable as they really are, what thrills one would get in playing this hole! What pleasurable excitement there would be in seeing one's second shot sailing over Hell!

It may be, however, that it is just as well these bunkers are blind. If they had been visible, although in reality they would

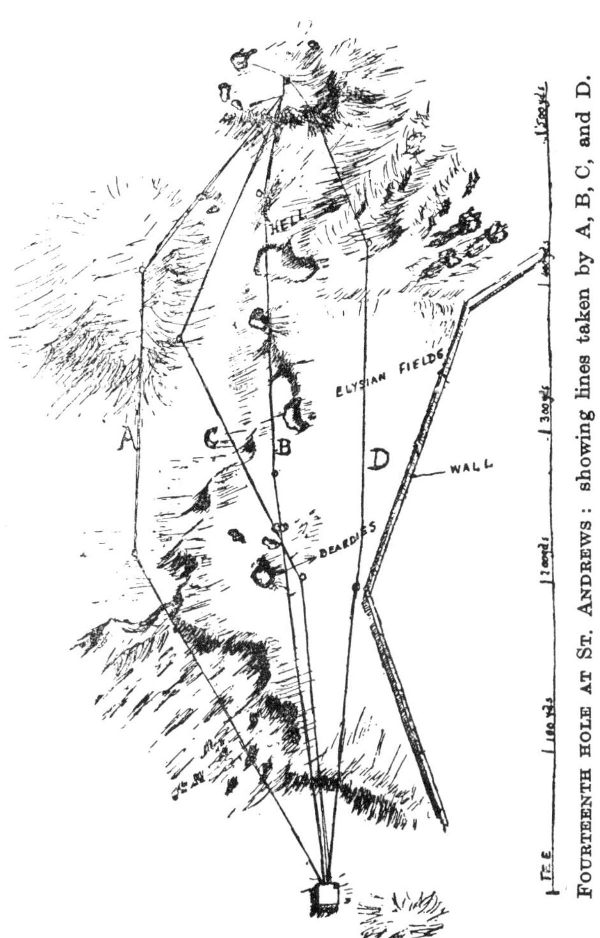

FOURTEENTH HOLE AT ST. ANDREWS: showing lines taken by A, B, C, and D.

have been much fairer, there would have been so many players crying out that it was most unfair that bunkers should be placed in the exact position where perfect shots go ; that it was most iniquitous to have a hazard like the Beardies 180 yards from the tee exactly in the line for the hole ; that the carry over Hell for the second shot is over 400 yards from the tee ; and that the only way to play the hole was along the fairway to the fifth, etc., etc.

As these bunkers are blind, players do not notice these things, and the lives of the Green Committee are saved.

The seventeenth hole at St. Andrews is almost too well known to need description—it is probably the most noted hole in the world. Although so difficult, it is by no means impossible for the long handicap player, for he can go pottering along, steering wide of all hazards, and losing strokes because he refuses to take any risks.

At this hole, once more, it is the slopes that give so much character to the hole. Even for the tee shot there is a ridge immediately beyond the corner of the station-master's garden which kicks your ball away from the hole if you pitch to the left of it, and towards the hole if you pitch to the right—in fact, an extra yard or two over the corner makes all the difference in getting into a favourable position for the second shot. There are also hillocks and ridges down the right-hand side, all forcing an inaccurately placed shot into an unfavourable position for the approach.

I often think that the hole would be more interesting without the Scholar's Bunker—the latter prevents a badly hit second getting into the danger zone. If it were not there, one would much more frequently be forced to play the sporting approach to the green with the road bunker intervening. It is this road bunker, with the slopes leading a ball to it, which makes this hole of such intense interest. Notwithstanding the abuse showered on it, this bunker has done more to sustain the popularity of St. Andrews than any feature on the course.

During the last few years there have been many good inland courses constructed. Several of these, such as Swinley Forest, St. George's Hill, Sunningdale, Alwoodley, Moortown, Ganton, etc., have some excellent long holes.

At Alwoodley, two of the dog-legged holes, the eighth and fifteenth, are particularly good examples. The eighth is played from right to left and the fifteenth from left to right. In each case the green has been constructed with a marked side slope, so that the nearer the golfer plays to the angle of the dog-leg, the greater the slope favours him.

In 1914 the writer designed an ideal two-shot hole which won the first prize in

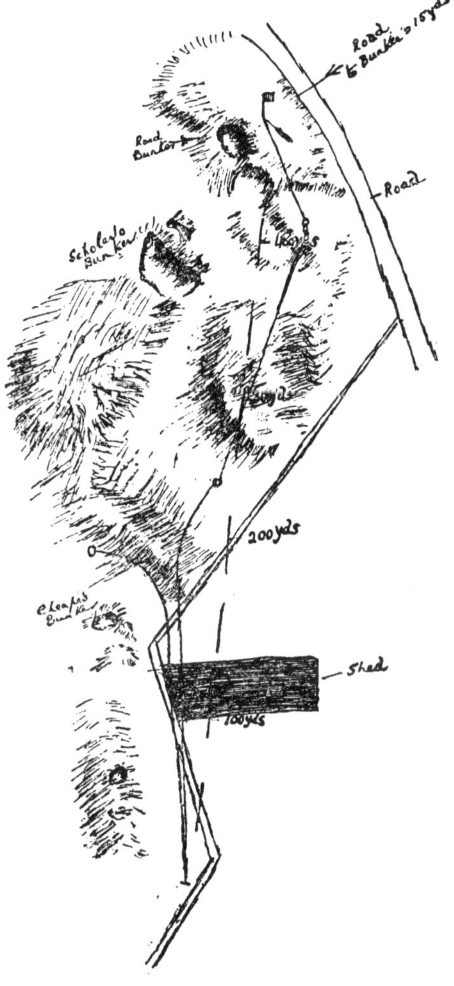

THE SEVENTEENTH HOLE AT ST. ANDREWS.

a competition for Golfing Architecture, promoted by *Country Life*.

In designing it, he attempted to produce an ideal hole among perfect surroundings, and what could be more perfect than sand-dunes by the seashore!

The hole is 420 yards long from the ordinary and 450 yards from the Medal Tee.

An effort has been made to produce the old type of golf, in which a player has no fixed line to the hole, but has to use his own judgment in playing it, according to varying conditions of wind, etc.

The green is guarded by bunkers and a large hillock (20 feet high) on the right of the approach, and is also tilted upwards from left to right and from the front to the back, so that the approach from the left is an easy one, and from the right necessitates such a difficult pitch that the player is likely to overrun the green into the bunker beyond.

There are five possible routes to the hole, and the choice of the player must vary from day to day, according to his length of drive, the state of the weather, etc.

It caters for all classes of players—even the absolute beginner can take No. 5 line. He loses strokes not by getting into bunkers, but by avoiding risks, and probably takes five, or at least four, to reach the green in consequence; nevertheless he enjoys his game, and not being disheartened, he improves, until finally he may be able to achieve the boldest line of all, and drive a fine ball straight to the hole.

He who takes the left-hand road by way of the island can also get home in two; he has a shorter carry, but has to make up for this by extreme accuracy.

There are many positions by the seashore where a hole of this kind could be constructed, but it would be possible to make one of a similar type inland, especially if the subsoil consisted of sand and the lie of the land was favourable. The seashore could be replaced by bunkers, old quarry workings, hummocky ground, rough, or even land out of bounds.

Success in construction depends entirely on expert supervision. It is like all successful golf-course construction, a question of making the best use of natural features and the devising of artificial ones, indistinguishable from nature.

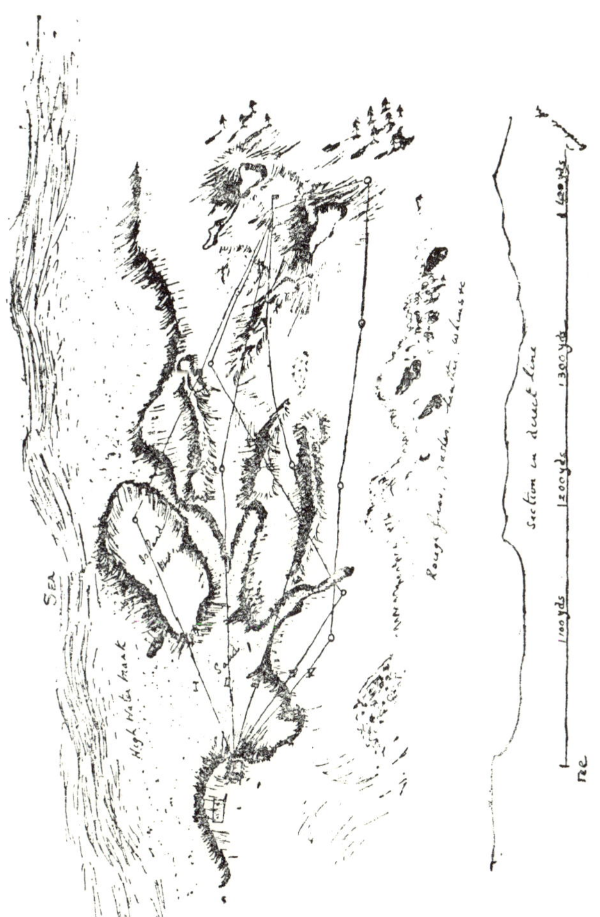

PLAN OF IDEAL TWO-SHOT HOLE OF 420 YARDS.

CHAPTER IV

THE FUTURE OF GOLF ARCHITECTURE

As the future of Golf Architecture depends on the prospects of golf, it may be of interest to discuss the probability of its abiding popularity.

Golf has been played in Scotland for several centuries, and there appears to be no sign of any decreased popularity, but rather the reverse. The illusiveness of golf is sufficient to ensure its popularity. No one ever seems to master it. You imagine you have got the secret to-day, but it has gone to-morrow. This is so in all good games. There are some games, such as ping-pong and roller-skating, which become merely passing crazes, and the reason is that one obtains a certain standard which neither diminishes nor increases, and then the game becomes monotonous. Golf on a first-rate course can never become monotonous, and the better the course the less likely it is to do so. Golf on a good links is, in all probability, the best game in the world, but on the late-Victorian type of inland course, where there is a complete lack of variety, flat fairways, flat unguarded greens, long grass, necessitating frequent searching for lost balls, and mathematically placed hazards consisting of the cop or pimple variety, it not only offends all the finest instincts of the artist and the sportsman, but is the most boring game in existence. The advent of the golf architect is rapidly curing all these disabilities.

A good golf course is a great asset to the nation. Those who harangue against land being diverted from agriculture and used for golf have little sense of proportion. Comparing the small amount of land utilised for golf with the large amount devoted to agriculture, we get infinitely more value out of the former than the latter. We all eat too much. During the Great War the majority were all the fitter for being rationed and getting a smaller amount of food, but none of us get enough fresh air, pleasurable excitement, and exercise. Health and happiness are everything in this world. Money-grubbing (so called business), except in so far as it helps to attain these, is of minor importance. One of the reasons why I, " a medical man," decided to give up medicine and take to golf architecture was my firm conviction of the extraordinary influence on health of pleasurable excitement, especially when combined with fresh air and exercise. How frequently have I, with great difficulty, persuaded patients who were never off my doorstep to take up golf, and how rarely, if ever, have I seen them in my consulting-rooms again! It is not suggested that golf is the one and only remedy. Men may get equal results from shooting, fishing, riding, cricket, tennis, etc., and may even obtain pleasurable excitement from gardening, politics, or their own business, but for the majority of men, golf is the most convenient form of pleasurable excitement and exercise to take. Those who rave against golf courses surely forget that many of the greatest politicians, thinkers, and business men conserve their health and their mental powers through golf. As examples we could quote President Wilson, Lloyd George, Carnegie, A. J. Balfour, Asquith, Winston Churchill, Lord Northcliffe, and scores of others. I hope to live to see the day when there are crowds of municipal courses, as in Scotland, cropping up all over England. It would help enormously in increasing the health, the virility, and the prosperity of the nation, and would do much to counteract discontent and Bolshevism. There can be no possible reason against, and there is every reason in favour of, municipal courses. They are all for the good of the community, and even from a financial point of view, at the small green fees of 3*d.* or 6*d.* a round invariably pay.

If this be so that games, and particularly golf, are of such vital importance to national health and social content, then surely the provision of adequate and proper facilities for golf should be taken seriously, and in making this provision the golf architect has a special part.

The test of a good golf architect is the power of converting bad inland material into a good course, and not the power of fashioning excellent seaside material into a mediocre one.

The majority of amateurs are sportsmen, and they welcome anything that increases the sporting element of the game. There are, on the other hand, others, including some of our best players, who look upon golf in the "card and pencil" spirit, and view with resentment anything that has stopped their steady series of threes and fours.

The advent of the golf architect has done much to increase the sporting and the dramatic element in golf. The true test of the value of his work is its popularity, and judging by the rapid increase in members, even on the mere rumour that the services of a well-known course architect are to be obtained, there can be no doubt the modern constructor of courses has achieved this. The writer knows examples of the reconstruction of one or two short holes bringing in over one hundred fresh members to a club which had been steadily diminishing in numbers for years.

There are many and varied qualities required for the making of a successful golf architect.

In the first place, he must have an

intimate knowledge of the theory of playing the game. He need not be himself a good player. He may have some physical disability which prevents him becoming so, but as the training of the golf architect is purely mental and not physical, this should not prevent him from being a successful golf-course architect. In any case, the possession of a vivid imagination, which is an absolute essential in obtaining success, may prevent him attaining a position among the higher ranks of players. Every one knows how fatal imagination is in playing the game. Let the fear of socketing once enter your head, and you promptly socket every shot afterwards.

His knowledge of the game should be so intimate that he knows instinctively what is likely to produce good golf and good golfers. He must have more than a passing acquaintance with the best courses and the best golfing holes. It is not only necessary that he should play them, but study them and analyse the features which make them what they are. He must have a sense of proportion and be able to differentiate between essentials and non-essentials. He should be able to distinguish between those features which are of supreme importance in the making of a hole and those which are of less value.

He must have judgment in the choice of features which can be readily and cheaply reproduced, and not those which are impossible to construct without an inordinate expenditure of labour.

How frequently has one seen hundreds of pounds wasted in a futile attempt to reproduce the Alps, the Himalayas, or the Cardinal! Features of this kind look absolutely out of place unless the surrounding ranges of hills which harmonise with them are also reproduced. To do this would involve the expenditure of hundreds of thousands of pounds. How often are attempts made to copy a hole and the subtle slopes and undulations which are the making of the original overlooked!

The golf-course architect must have the sporting instinct, and if he has had a training in many and varied branches of sport, and has analysed those characteristics which provide a maximum of pleasurable excitement in them, so much the better. It is essential that he should eliminate his own game entirely, and look upon all constructional work in a purely impersonal manner.

He should be able to put himself in the position of the best player that ever lived, and at the same time be extremely sympathetic towards the beginner and long handicap player.

He should, above all, have a sense of proportion and be able to come to a prompt decision as to what is the greatest good to the greatest number.

THE FIFTH HOLE AT FULFORD, YORKS—APPROXIMATE COST, £35: the whole of the additional nine holes on this course were constructed on dead flat land at a total cost of about £300.

He should not be unduly influenced by hostile criticism, but should give the most sympathetic consideration to criticism of a constructive nature. Not infrequently a long handicap man makes a brilliant suggestion which can often be utilised in a modified form.

A knowledge of psychology gained in the writer's medical training has been of great service in estimating what is likely to give the greatest pleasure to the greatest number.

It by no means follows that what appears to be attractive at first sight will be permanently so. A good golf course grows on one like good painting, good music, etc.

The ideal golf architect should have made a study, from a golfing point of view, of agricultural chemistry, botany, and geology. He should also have some knowledge of surveying, map-reading, and the interpretation of aerial photographs.

Aerial photography will become of enormous value in all kinds of surveying, town-planning, the construction of golf courses, etc.

There are all sorts of details visible in an aerial photograph which are often omitted after the most careful survey in the ordinary way. The exact positions of every tree, hummock, natural bunker, tracks, hedges, ditches, etc., are well defined. The exact areas occupied by permanent pasture, grass grown for hay, crops, clumps of whins, rushes, etc., can all be distinguished in an aerial photograph.

These, combined with a good ordnance and geological drift-map, are of inestimable value, and in many cases would assist even the most expert golf architect to make such full use of all the natural features that thousands of pounds might ultimately be saved in reducing the acreage required and in minimising the cost of labour, upkeep, etc.

In these days when manual labour costs so much, it is of supreme importance to reduce it to a minimum by the substitution of mental labour.

Golf architecture is a new art closely allied to that of the artist or the sculptor, but also necessitating a scientific knowledge of many other subjects.

In the old days, many golf courses were designed by prominent players, who after a preliminary inspection of the course simply placed pegs to represent the position of the sites for the suggested tees, greens, bunkers, etc. The whole thing was completed in a few hours, and the best results could hardly have been expected, and in fact never were obtained, by these methods.

The modern designer, on the other hand, is likely to achieve the most perfect results and make the fullest use of all the natural features by more up-to-date methods.

After a preliminary inspection or inspections in the calm and quiet of his own study with an ordnance map and, if possible, aeroplane photographs in front of him, he visualises every feature. He is then not so likely to be obsessed by details, but gives everything its due proportionate value. He then evolves his scheme and pays a second visit to the ground, and, if necessary, modifies his ideas according to the appearance on the spot.

There is an extraordinary resemblance between what is now known as the camouflage of military earthworks and golf-course construction.

The writer was fortunate during the war in being asked to give the demonstrations to members of the Army Council which were the foundation of, and led to the establishment of, the first school of camouflage.

These demonstrations were evolved from

his experience as a golf-course architect in the imitation of natural features.

Successful golf-course construction and successful camouflage are almost entirely due to utilisation of natural features to the fullest extent and to the construction of artificial ones indistinguishable from nature.

It is clear that if a gun emplacement or any other object of military importance is made indistinguishable from the most innocent-looking feature on the landscape, it will escape the disagreeable attention of the enemy. And what can appear more innocent than the natural undulations of the ground? Therefore in camouflage, as in golf-course construction, the ability to imitate natural undulations successfully is of special importance.

There are many other attributes in common between the successful golf architect and the camoufleur.

Both, if not actually artists, must have

an artistic temperament, and have had an education in science.

Surprise is the most important thing in war, and by camouflage you are able to obtain this not only on the defence but in the attack.

In golf architecture and camouflage a knowledge of psychology is of enormous value. It enables one to judge what is likely to give pleasurable excitement to the golfer and confidence and improvement in *moral* to the soldier. The writer feels most strongly that his experience in the Great War in visualising and surveying miles of sites for fortifications in this country and abroad, in map-reading, in the interpretation of aerial photographs, in drainage and labour-saving problems, and particularly in the mental training of strategic camouflage and devising traps and surprises for the enemy, was by no means wasted even from a golf-course point of view. The only man he has been successful in initiating rapidly into the mysteries of golf-course architecture was not a golfer but an artist, and one of the greatest, if not the greatest, of experts on camouflage.

A little knowledge is a specially dangerous thing in links' architecture. One of our greatest troubles in dealing with the committees of the old-established seaside courses is that their world-renowned reputation (not due to any virtue of their own, but entirely owing to the natural advantages of their links) makes them think themselves competent judges of a golf course.

They ask for a report and plan of suggested improvements, and then imagine they have grasped the ideas of the designer, and proceed to make a horrible hash of it. I do not know a single seaside course which has been remodelled in anything like the way it should have been remodelled.

The best artificially constructed seaside course I know is the Eden (Mr. Colt's) Course at St. Andrews. There are few of the crowds of players who, notwithstanding its youth, already congregate on it realise how much is due to artificiality and how little to nature. All the best ground at St. Andrews had been previously seized for the three older courses—viz., the Old, the New, and the Jubilee—and yet it compares favourably with any of them. This is entirely due to the fact that not only was it designed by Mr. Colt, but the construction work was done by men who had been trained under him and worked under his supervision.

It is much better that construction work should be done by men without any knowledge of the subject than by those partly trained.

There is a yarn told about two rival constructors of golf courses: one of them was admiring the other's greens, and remarked that " he never managed to get his green-keeper to make the undulations as natural looking." The other replied that " it was perfectly easy ; he simply employed the biggest fool in the village and told him to make them flat."

I believe the real reason St. Andrews Old Course is infinitely superior to anything else is owing to the fact that it was constructed when no one knew anything about the subject at all, and since then it has been considered two sacred to be touched. What a pity it is that the natural advantages of many seaside courses have been neutralised by bad designing and construction work !

The architect is the best judge in deciding how often he should visit a course for supervision purposes. How often have I heard from the secretary, who is almost invariably a cheery optimist, that the construction work was going on splendidly, and when too late discovered that hundreds of pounds had been thrown away in doing bad work which had ultimately to be scrapped!

There is an old Persian saying:

> "He who knows not, and knows not that he knows not, is a fool. Avoid him.
>
> "He who knows not, and knows that he knows not will learn. Teach him.
>
> "He who knows, and knows not that he knows, will fail. Pity him.
>
> "He who knows, and knows that he knows, is a wise man. Follow him."

The majority of committees, being composed of men who have made their living out of their brains, are beginning to know that they know not, and this is all to the good of the future of golf.

The most backward committees are those in Scotland, London, and America. They have not yet realised that golf-course architecture is a question of mental and not physical training. It is particularly strange that my own countrymen, who have such a wealth of golfing material and attach so much importance to education, attach so little to education in golf architecture.

The time will surely come, as it has already done in the North of England, when committees will attach as much importance to the architecture of the course as to that of the club-house.

In time many of the dull, monotonous, muddy inland London links will be entirely remodelled under expert supervision, and the turf and subsoil treated so that it is a pleasure to play on them even during the winter months.

The time will also come when even some of the championship courses will be entirely remodelled under expert supervision, and when these clubs will realise how little they have made of the natural advantages that Providence has provided for them.

Printed in Great Britain
by Hazell, Watson & Viney, Ld., London and Aylesbury,
for Simpkin, Marshall, Hamilton, Kent & Co., Ltd.

Afterword
by
Lewis A. Lapham

I first met Dr. MacKenzie on the first tee of the newly incorporated Cypress Point Golf Club in the late summer of 1927, just before I went off to my college freshman year. He was, as I recall, a balding, stocky, somewhat saturnine man in plus fours, then in his late fifties. I don't believe I ever saw him again after our work together.

To the best of a memory increasingly flawed over, and by, the sixty intervening years, Dr. MacKenzie's basic work on the golf course was already done. The fairways, the greens, the traps, and most of the tees were in place, and the seeding was begun.

The Club was conceived, I think, by Marion Hollins, the 1921 Women's National Amateur champion. Later, she was selling real estate on the Monterey Peninsula and, with my father and several others, put together the syndicate that bought the original 170 acres for $150,000 from the Del Monte Properties Company.

It was almost certainly Miss Hollins who suggested the first architect for Cypress Point, Seth J. Raynor, a long-time associate of Charles Blair Macdonald. Macdonald and Raynor, together and separately, had designed a number of distinguished layouts, including the Na-

tional Golf Links at Southampton, Sleepy Hollow on the Hudson, Mid-Ocean in Bermuda, Waialae at Honolulu, Fishers Island, Yale Golf Club, et al.

Raynor died just as he was to begin at Cypress, and Dr. MacKenzie came in, again I think, at the suggestion of Miss Hollins. He was a retired British Army surgeon turned camouflage expert turned golf architect, and he had already built courses in England, Ireland, Scotland, New Zealand, and Australia, most notably Royal Melbourne, and, later, he was to do one of his most famous courses in collaboration with Bobby Jones—the Augusta National, home of the Masters.

Shortly into the first chapter of his "Golf Architecture", MacKenzie considers "the essential features of an ideal golf course" and sets forth thirteen precepts.

One of them proposes that "there should be a sufficient number of heroic carries from the tee, but the course should be arranged so that the weaker player . . . shall always have an alternate route open to him."

That is how I came to meet him.

I was by 1927 standards (wooden shafts) a big hitter and, by any year's standards, a very wild one. However, the Doctor was a patient man. He used me to measure the extent of the "heroic carry".

Although MacKenzie had settled on the sites of most of the tees, he was not sure about five or six of them. I specifically remember numbers two, eight, sixteen, and seventeen. If you know the course, you will know why. Each of these tees, most spectacularly the sixteenth, offers the big hitter a sporting chance which, if successfully taken, returns a handsome reward. The player who fails is ferociously penalized. Each of the four holes also gives the weaker player a safe alternative, although I suppose safe is a relative term, notably at number eight. The alternative there is skimpy.

We spent the better part of four or five mornings more or less in the vicinity of the present tees on those holes. The Doctor had a small portable mat for me to hit from and two men out yonder to measure my drives. He would put the mat down, seat himself on a shooting stick, and tell me to hit away, laddie.

My first three or four tee shots were generally in the spinach, but, as I say, the Doctor was a patient man. When I finally flushed one, he'd move the mat five, ten, fifteen yards right, left, up, back, or wherever, and we'd go at it again, seventy or eighty balls a morning. We spent a lot of time at number seventeen, moving way out toward the ocean to the right of the present tee. And I think, but cannot be sure, that he and I tried a couple of possible tee positions up the dunes above the present tees for holes twelve and thirteen.

I have heard that Dr. MacKenzie toyed with the idea of making number sixteen a par 4, and indeed the preliminary map he gave the Club in February, 1926, sketches two such par 4 alternatives. But, when I met him, he was about to settle, happily I think, for the present hole, surely one of the most famous par 3s extant and perhaps the most photographed.

That same map, a drawing of which is in the appendix to this book, shows a number of other variations from the present course. What is now the 493-yard par-5 fifth is shown as a 439-yard par 4, over the same general route. The present 518-yard par-5 sixth was originally two separate holes, a 140-yard par 3 (number six) and a 360-yard par 4 (number seven). The present number seven, a fine 165-yard par 3 from an elevated tee across a deep swale to a heavily trapped elevated green at the foot of a huge dune, was not shown at all. What is now the 404-yard par-4 twelfth is first sketched as a

550-yard par 5 into the usually prevailing head wind, followed by a 130-yard par 3 as against the present 365-yard par-4 thirteenth.

It is possible that Raynor had roughly routed the course before his death and that MacKenzie used Raynor's plan for his original presentation, but that is pure supposition. A better guess, I think, is that MacKenzie drew his own rough plan after a preliminary walkabout and only got down to cases when he later came fully to recognize the land's potential. Hence, for example, the creation of the present seventh hole.

But all this is rank speculation on my part and, whichever it was, the course is clearly MacKenzie's, ably assisted during his absences on work elsewhere by Robert Hunter, an able designer in his own right.

If you will turn back to MacKenzie's thirteen "essential features", you will find virtually all of them beautifully demonstrated at Cypress Point, notably his idea about "artificial features". "These," he said, "should have so natural an appearance that a stranger is unable to distinguish them from nature itself." I have never spotted an artificial feature on the course in all the years I have played it, and I challenge you to.

The sole exception to the MacKenzie canon,

as I see it, is his tenth "essential feature", i.e. "there should be a complete absence of the annoyance and irritation caused by the necessity of searching for lost balls". The good Doctor must here have overlooked ice plant, saw grass, and huge acreages of unraked and scruffily overgrown dunes.

I know nothing about golf course design, but it has always seemed to me that the fewer changes required over the years to keep a course in excellent playing condition, the more gilt-edged the course's original values. In a copy of a book on golf architecture by Wethered and Simpson, which MacKenzie presented to the Club in 1930, he scribbled in the margin of one of the pages: "A golf course that is altered is an indication of faulty design". If there is anything in this premise, Cypress Point can hold its head high. The changes have been minimal.

The present fourth tee lies about fifteen yards to the left of the original. I believe MacKenzie would like the change. It brings the left-side fairway bunkers into stronger position to fulfill his precept of the "heroic carry".

The present ninth tee is about ten yards below and fifteen yards behind the original, which was on the upper shelf of the existing eighth green. The tee was moved to protect golfers driving from number nine against errant approach shots of those playing up to number eight.

The original fifteenth tee, now the shorter option, has been replaced by a tee considerably farther back and set below on a ledge directly above a narrow, swirling, rocky channel of the Pacific. It is a dandy perch in April from which to watch harbor seal mothers teaching their pups to swim, and an occasional sea otter or two.

Only one of the original eighteen greens has been re-contoured and that is number eight, which was stretched to take up the space left by the removal of the original ninth tee.

Of the original one hundred and twenty-five traps, about thirty have been eliminated. Most had more drainage or other maintenance problems than they were worth. In the early years there were clusters of shallow traps surrounding the small groves of cypress trees in the middle of the first and seventeenth fairways. These traps were, I think, largely cosmetic, for if you hit your shot into the trees you had about all the penalty you deserved without having additionally to compete with the sand. A chain of traps across the fourteenth fairway vanished long ago, mainly, I suspect, because it invariably caught the best tee shot of the president of the Club.

A sad and heavy number of the cypress trees for which the point was named are also long gone, fallen to age or wind. Many of their bare and twisted trunks remain, however, looking for all the world like an alfresco exhibition of modern sculpture.

I sometimes wonder whether MacKenzie, who died in 1934, would want to change his course today, given the strength and length of the top modern players. Perhaps he would seek to add several hundred yards to Cypress Point's present 6506 yards, which makes it the next-to-the-shortest of the fifty-eight courses on the PGA Tour. (Those figures are taken from a recently published book, "Golf Courses of the PGA Tour", by George Peper, editor of Golf Magazine. *Parenthetically, its dust jacket shows a player driving from the sixteenth at Cypress.)*

On the other hand, the same table of figures, compiled from 1983 through 1985, shows that Cypress ranked as the fifth toughest course on the Tour. Of the eight hundred and twenty-eight toughest holes assessed, number sixteen at

Cypress ranked first, number fourteen ranked seventh, and number eight ranked tenth.

Dr. MacKenzie can rest easy.

Obviously the place stirs up a lot of memories for me. The ashes of both my parents are buried on a small knoll not far from the first green. Another great and good friend, Francis McComas, is buried on the edge of the Pacific to the right of the path leading from the fifteenth green to the sixteenth tee. McComas, an artist, had much to do with the interior design of the club house, itself almost unchanged since it was completed in 1930.

I have seen a lot of golf played at Cypress, from the sublime to the ludicrous, a fair portion of the latter produced by myself. At the other end of the spectrum, I was unhappily partnered in a fivesome against Tommy Armour during Christmas week, 1930, and watched him shoot a 29 on the last nine holes of a 72-hole match, including a hole-in-one at number fifteen. A few years later, when I had a match going with Pete Bostwick, a polo player of note, I saw him knock in an ace at the short par-4 number nine (pin on lower level). Playing in the foursome ahead of him, I had just holed a chip shot for a two and was standing smugly at the top of the green counting my money. At that point Bostwick cut loose, and I can still see his tee shot landing ten or twelve yards short of the pin and rolling up and in. I felt as though a surgeon had just told me that I had to have my gallbladder out, and I have never trusted a polo player since. And three or four years ago, playing behind Howard Clark, a former president of the U.S. Seniors, I watched him play the last four holes in ten shots.

I don't know whether Armour's 29 has been equalled, though, given the quality of today's leading players, I would not fall out of my chair if someone has done so. But if anyone else knocks in his tee shot at number nine or finishes 2-2-4-2, I will eat the chair.

As to the Cypress Point Golf Club itself, its first yearbook, 1928, shows a list of one hundred and three members. By 1933, the number had dwindled to perhaps forty-five, the result to some extent of the economic fall-out that began in October, 1929. The Club was, to be blunt, all but broke. The Del Monte Properties Company, under the chairmanship of the generous and far-sighted S.F.B. Morse, in effect carried the Club through World War II. The situation turned around thereafter, the membership began to grow, and guest cards multiplied. The

Club has been very much a going proposition ever since.

Grantland Rice, the leading sportswriter of his era, came west to cover the U.S. Amateur championship at Pebble Beach in 1929, the first time the venue was west of the Mississippi. He toured Cypress a time or two and shortly thereafter wrote the following appraisal:

"This new course or links will be a fine test of golf, and in addition it will have golf character and a scenic flare which will place it upon the peak. You can label it sensational, dramatic, spectacular or what you will, and still fall short of any worthy description. The dunes, the cypress, and the sea round out a setting which so far is unparalled in golf from Scotland to the Riviera, from Maine to Mexico."

Dr. MacKenzie made Rice a true prophet.

Lewis A. Lapham

Appendix

Cypress Point Golf Club Prospectus, 1928, including the original MacKenzie layout and photographs of the sites for various holes and greens. Reprinted with the kind permission of the Cypress Point Golf Club.

INTRODUCTION

The Monterey Peninsula has ideal terrain and climate for the development of all outdoor sports. The facilities for the enjoyment of these sports have been developed to a very high degree by the Del Monte Properties Company. There are now three golf links on the Peninsula, and a fourth will be built within a year.

It is now proposed to organize a club to acquire property that is generally referred to as Cypress Point, and to construct thereon a golf links for the use of members only. The site of this club is extraordinary, both from a scenic standpoint and from its natural adaptability to the game. It is doubtful if any more desirable terrain for a golf course exists in the world. This is a broad assertion to make, but innumerable golfers who have played the game in various parts of the globe have been authority for this statement. It has been stated by Seth Raynor and by Dr. Mackenzie that it would be possible to build the greatest golf course in the world in that particular locality.

CYPRESS POINT GOLF CLUB

Executive Committee

W. W. Crocker
Fred W. Flint, Jr.
Kenneth R. Kingsbury

Miss Marion Hollins
Harry H. Hunt
Mrs. Wm. C. Van Antwerp

Roger D. Lapham, Chairman

Miss Marion Hollins has secured from the Del Monte Properties Company an option on about 170 acres of land including what is known as Cypress Point on the Monterey Peninsula. An express condition of this option is that Miss Hollins will cause to be organized a social and athletic club with articles of incorporation and by-laws in form and substance satisfactory to the Del Monte Properties Company and with a membership of not less than 100 and a paid capital of not less than $200,000. When this club is organized, Miss Hollins is to assign her interest in the option to that Club, and the Club is then required to start building a golf links within six months.

On condition that this 170 acres of land be used as indicated, Del Monte Properties Company has quoted a price of $150,000. payable in installments as follows: If and when the work of constructing the golf course is completed, the payment of any portion of the $150,000. may be deferred for five years, except that $50,000. must be paid on the expiration of five years, and the balance within ten years. Interest on deferred payments at the rate of six per cent.

It is proposed that a very attractive club house be constructed, which will have many comfortable bedrooms, dining room,

Sitting rooms, etc.

The land was first laid out for a golf links by Mr. Seth Raynor, Associate Golf Architect with Mr. Charles B. Macdonald. After Mr. Raynor's death, Miss Hollins was fortunate in securing the services of Dr. Alister MacKenzie of England to complete the plan of the links. Dr. MacKenzie has constructed over three hundred English and Scotch courses and has stated that "Cypress Point has interested me more than any land I have ever had to deal with. For the sake of my reputation, I should like to make you the best golf links in existence."

In considering membership in this Club, the salient points are as follows:

(1) The price of $150,000. is perhaps one-fifth of a conservative value of the ground. This price and terms, however, are made because of the fact that the property is to be used as a golf links.

(2) Membership at the present time is comparable with that of any of the other proprietary clubs in the State, in their initial period. Purely as an investment, a study of the other prominent golf clubs will convince one that a membership in this club, limited as it is, will be very valuable in the very near future. The development of the Monterey Peninsula as a residential area has been very rapid, and the next few years will show a far greater scope of building and development. This means a great demand for memberships in what will be the most exclusive golf club owning the best golf links in the State of California.

(3) While the principal object of the club is the development

of the golf links, the club will have an attractive home, which will offer all the accomodations and attractions of a country club. There will also be facilities for tennis, bathing and other outdoor sports.

(4) The golf links and club will be located in the Del Monte Forest, and members will have the use of the vast system of bridle paths, private roads and other attractions of that area. Also, the club is only five minutes from Pebble Beach Lodge and twenty minutes from Hotel Del Monte.

(5) Owing to the extraordinary terms of purchase, no cash is required for the ground at this time. It is therefore perfectly safe for 100 members to start construction of the golf links. No payments are necessary on principal for a five year period. The estimates of cost shown in the following statement are very liberal, and represent the final liability of the club with 250 members.

INVESTED VALUE

Cost of 170 acres of land	$ 150,000
Cost of club house	150,000
Construction of golf links	150,000
Incidental items	50,000
Total Cost	$ 500,000
250 memberships at $2,000.	$ 500,000

ESTIMATED ANNUAL MAINTENANCE

Upkeep of golf links	$ 32,000
Repairs to club house & loss on restaurant	6,000
Taxes	4,500
Maintenance of roads	2,500
Salary of Professional	5,000
Estimated cost of maintenance	$ 50,000

DESCRIPTION OF PLATES ILLUSTRATING CYPRESS POINT LINKS.

No. 1. This aeroplane view of the proposed course was drawn by Albert Barrows from the sketches and plans prepared by Dr. MacKenzie. Although reproduced on a small scale, the reader can get a very good idea of the unexampled terrain surrounding the various holes.

In the first place it should be noted that the white foreground is not sand but forest. The more darkly shaded ground in the righthand corner comprises the pure white sand dunes which have been noted by anyone who has taken the Seventeen Mile Drive.

The fairways of the holes from the first to the fifth lie almost wholly within the confines of the forest. From the sixth tee the player drives directly into the face of one of these magnificent white mountains of sand. The holes from the seventh to the thirteenth are played directly in the dunes and thereby exactly reproduce the conditions found in the famous seaside championship links of Great Britain.

The fourteenth, starting the player on the edge of the sand dunes, takes him directly along the edge of the forest into a green situated within a stone's throw of the ocean spray.

It is hard to avoid superlatives in describing this course but certainly the next three holes are spectacular and bold beyond all imagining. Some idea may be gained from the following plates 9 to 13.

No. 2. The club house site is on a raise that overlooks the forest on one side, Fan Shell Beach and Cypress Point on the other.

No. 3. Setting which seems to have been formed by nature as an ideal location for the first green.

No. 4. Natural hazards which border the fairway going to the fifth hole.

No. 5. View taken from point above the 9th green. The line of play comes from the righthand side. At the extreme left of the picture beneath the Cypress tree is the location of the fourteenth green.

No. 6. Setting for the ninth green.

No. 7. Here is some real "tiger country" that will entrap the sliced approach to the 12th.

No. 8. Fourteenth fairway. Line of play from left to right.

No. 9. View from the fifteenth tee showing the character of ground that must be carried on this short pitch shot.

No. 10. Location of the fifteenth green. This view was taken from the back of the green looking towards the tee, which is perched on the clift in the center of the picture.

No. 11. Looking towards Cypress Point giving general view of sixteenth and seventeenth holes.

No. 12. Facing the green from the sixteenth tee. This will be a par 3 hole which will call for a carry of somewhere from 185 to 200 yards. The feeling of satisfaction after a successful shot here will surpass that of the player who has triumphantly negotiated the famous carry at the eighth or Chasm hole at Pebble Beach.

PACIFIC OCEAN
15
14
1
16
17
18
Cypress Point
Golf Links

This map represents MacKenzie's original 1926 layout for the Cypress Point links. Changes made during construction are detailed on the following page.

Explanation of Map

The map on the preceeding pages, dated 1928, represents the proposed Cypress Point course "drawn by Albert Barrows from the sketches and plans prepared by Dr. MacKenzie," some of which date from 1926. Although this early version is close to the final product, the changes MacKenzie made as he went from the drawing board to construction illustrate the necessity of the architect seeing his course through its construction phase if, that is, he is interested in a superior product.

On the first nine MacKenzie changed the map's par-4 fifth hole into the par 5 of today which dog-legs left and uphill. He combined the map's par-3 sixth and par-4 seventh into today's sixth—a 518 yard par 5 which swings left and downhill, not unlike what he was later to do with the second at Augusta National. The tee on today's splendid 168 yard par-3 seventh hole is positioned after the map's seventh hole, with the green up in the sandhills toward the map's directional arrow. He then moved the map's eighth tee up the hill to be near the new seventh green, creating an exciting blind tee-shot and sharp dog-leg right, and in doing so designed one of the world's great par 4s, a hole which beautifully illustrates many of MacKenzie's architectural principles.

On the second nine he converted the map's par 5 eleventh and twelfth holes into par 4s, producing another masterpiece in today's 404-yard twelfth, with its echoes of the tremendous fifth at Royal County Down. He lengthened the map's thirteenth, now that he had a shorter twelfth, from a par 3 into today's lovely medium-length par 4. MacKenzie's idea of setting the tee to the eighteenth on a rocky promintory in the ocean proved unfeasable (he drew intricate plans for a footbridge over the water), so he moved the tee to the shore and situated the green farther up the hill next to the clubhouse.

The Cypress Point course has undergone extremely few changes and is almost identical to the course MacKenzie completed in 1929.

Cypress Point, Clubhouse site

Site for First green, typical Scottish 'links' country

Cypress bordered fairways for Fifth hole

Typical Cypress Point land, view from above site for Ninth green

Cypress Point, Ninth green site

Through the sand dunes, site for the Ninth hole

From sand dunes to cliffs, site for the Fourteenth hole

Site for Fifteenth green to left and Sixteenth green in distance to right

Site for Fifteenth green

Site for Sixteenth green and Seventeenth tee in distance

Site for Sixteenth tee